Irena Macri was born in Ukraine and moved to Australia
at the age of sixteen. She graduated from the College of
Fine Arts at UNSW with a Bachelor of Digital Media.
In 2012, she founded the popular blog Eat Drink Paleo.

Irena is a digital nomad and an avid traveler.
She divides her time between London and Sydney.

Over 110 paleo-inspired recipes for everyone

EAT
DRINK

Paleo

COOKBOOK

IRENA MACRI

CHRONICLE BOOKS
SAN FRANCISCO

First published in the United States of America in 2016 by Chronicle Books LLC.
First published in Australia in 2013 by Penguin Random House Australia.

Library of Congress Cataloging-in-Publication Data available.
ISBN 978-1-4521-5223-3

33614059719723

Manufactured in China

Designed by Carla Hackett
Food and prop styling by Irena Macri
Typesetting by D.C. Type

10 9 8 7 6 5 4 3 2 1

Chronicle Books LLC
680 Second Street
San Francisco, California 94107
www.chroniclebooks.com

———— contents ————

Welcome

Thank you for purchasing my cookbook.
The fact that you did means that you
and I are very much alike—we enjoy
good food; we care about our well-being;
we love to cook; and we have fun in the
kitchen and outside of it. Perhaps you're
not all of the above, but I bet we could be
friends. So let me introduce myself and
tell you a little story of how this cookbook
came to be.

my journey

It all started in May 2012, when I quit my corporate job to pursue a passion—read: obsession—for cooking and all the other things that qualify me as a life-long foodie. Yes, I know, there are millions of other people who share the same passion—hello, *MasterChef* and Food Network—but I'm talking about a slightly different fixation. What I have, and I've had it ever since I cooked my first dish in my grandmother's kitchen, is an insatiable desire to play with food—to whisk it, mold it, whip it, sizzle it, and drizzle it till the cows come home. For a long time now, I've seen the kitchen as a playground where I can create and let my instincts go wild, where I can experiment and where I don't follow instructions. It's a feeling of wanting everyone else to see cooking through my eyes, and to show that it's completely normal to get stupidly excited about a truffle or a piece of amazing grass-fed beef or waking up in the middle of the night to write down a recipe I just dreamt about because I feel like it's the most brilliant one I've ever come up with and everyone will love it.

This "inner vocation" slowly grew into a nebulous dream, but for a long time I didn't know what to do with it. I left it there like a reserve batter, benched by the side of the playing field. I kept looking for an outlet, something to pour my passion for food into. I thought about going to a culinary school, opening my own wine bar or café, starting a catering business—and, yes, maybe for just one second, I imagined going on *MasterChef* or some other cooking contest. None of it sat well in my head or in my heart. I like to believe I'm a live-in-the-moment, be-free, make-your-own-rules kind of gal, and I just couldn't commit. Then I discovered paleo, a diet and lifestyle I will touch on in the next chapter, and everything fell into place. I found a way to combine my passion for cooking with my skills and background in digital media, and created something that allowed me to play by my own rules. My web site, Eat Drink Paleo, was born.

Focusing on paleo was a no-brainer for me—I was getting into the lifestyle and feeling fantastic as a result, and I was cooking a bunch of great food and trying new ingredients. At the same time, there was a lack of exciting, paleo-friendly recipes around. It was a perfect combination—an opportunity to unleash my culinary experiments and kitchen prowess; to learn and, consequently, educate others on how to feel great by eating real, delicious food. In addition, I felt the need to demystify paleo as a diet, which I thought was perceived as a fad or as a boring, impractical, restrictive, and meat-heavy way of eating. I knew firsthand that it doesn't have to be that way and that my approach—flexible, affirmative, and personal—was an easier way to integrate the paleo diet into one's life.

For nine months, I'd developed, tested, and photographed paleo-inspired recipes for my site, building a community, educating myself, and advocating good nutrition and healthier lifestyle habits. My audience grew quickly, and I knew I was on to something. You know you're doing something right when you start receiving emails and comments from real people telling you they had a fabulous dinner with their family thanks to your recipes, or that your content and passion inspires them on their journey.

I realized that I'd found a way to connect.

Making a cookbook was a natural progression. I had so many fantastic recipes in my head, and I really wanted to produce something that was different from what was available. I envisioned a cookbook that reflects my 80/20 philosophy, showcases real food and natural ingredients, and screams "cooking is fun!"

> My 80/20 philosophy . . .
>
> screams "cooking is fun!"

This cookbook is direct from the heart of someone who really loves to cook. It's been created in a very small kitchen, using basic equipment and common ingredients, demonstrating that the recipes can be cooked by pretty much anyone. It's also special because it was originally self-published and made possible by many friends and strangers who believed in my crazy dream and gave me an unbelievable opportunity to share it with you.

Irena xo

about the book

♥ My cookbook is for everyone—paleo, non-paleo, occasional cooks, *MasterChef* wannabes, moms, dads, and people living anywhere in the world. I tried to develop a variety of recipes, suitable for cooks of any level with an occasional advanced task or technique thrown in.

♥ All recipes featured in this cookbook are grain- and gluten-free, and contain no legumes, processed sugar, artificial ingredients, or chemicals.

♥ You will find that some of my recipes contain healthful, full-fat dairy and natural sweeteners; some are a little naughty and should be left for special occasions and consumed in moderation; and a few contain alcohol, because that's the way I like it—I enjoy it in moderation and in good company.

♥ Use this cookbook as an inspirational tool. Try ingredients you haven't cooked with before, follow the recipes but also play with and adapt my ideas to your own liking.

♥ My existing Eat Drink Paleo readers will notice that a small number of recipes are not new. That's because I wanted to include the most popular recipes from the web site in this cookbook for everyone to enjoy, and to have my "best of" in one place.

about me

- I was born in Ukraine, in a small city near the Carpathian Mountains. I moved to Australia when I was 16 years old.

- I had an unusually developed palate when I was a child. I was obsessed with *salo*, a type of Russian salty lard; loved herring, olives, salami, and liver pâté; and I even ate raw meat.

- Sydney, Australia, is my home, but I'm a bit of a digital nomad. I love Tuscany for food, Tonsai in Thailand for adventure, and Tokyo for all the craziness.

- I eat paleo 80 percent of the time, with the remaining 20 percent consisting of occasional butter, cheese, rice, quinoa, fresh corn, beer, dumplings, and gelato.

- I learned to cook from my family, through my travels, and by watching lots of cooking shows. I own a lot of cookbooks and food magazines, but I hardly ever cook from recipes.

- My foodie icons include Jamie Oliver, Maggie Beer, Lotta Lundgren, Nigella Lawson, Heston Blumenthal, and my inspiring late grandmother.

- My favorite ingredients are butter, garlic, lemon, olive oil, chiles, avocado, sweet potato, broccoli, gherkins, grass-fed beef, berries, coconut cream, and anything with truffles.

Tea time

Sand cupcakes

as you go along

Get familiar with these icons to help you navigate and filter through the recipes.

CONTAINS EGGS

CONTAINS NIGHTSHADES

CONTAINS DAIRY

CONTAINS NATURAL SWEETENERS

CONTAINS NUTS

CONTAINS SHELLFISH

CARB ALERT

UNDER 30 MINUTES

UNDER 1 HOUR

GREAT FOR ENTERTAINING

Recipes are divided into the following sections:

WAKE UP, BABY
Delicious, satiating food ideas to kick-start your day.

FROM THE GARDEN
Salads, soups, and sides made with vegetables, mushrooms, nuts, seeds, and fruits.

MEAT
Recipes using a variety of meats as the key ingredient.

FISH 'N' FRIENDS
Fish, shrimp, oysters, and much more.

CHEEKY TREATS
Desserts and sweet treats for special occasions, weekends, and entertaining.

QUICKIES
Snacks and small plates for parties and ideas for food on the go.

MAKE YOUR OWN
Make your own sauces, condiments, dips, stock, and yogurt.

BOTTOMS UP
Originals and paleo adaptations of the classic cocktails, shakes, and smoothies.

paleo know-how

ROBB WOLF I owe a lot of my paleo know-how to this guy. A former research biochemist, Robb wrote *New York Times* bestseller *The Paleo Solution: The Original Human Diet*, which was the book that convinced me to try paleo. I'm a regular listener of his highly entertaining weekly podcast and I often visit his web site when looking for nutrition and fitness information. I love his sensible approach and his sense of humor.

MARK SISSON The George Clooney of the paleo world, Mark is an American fitness author and blogger known for his book *The Primal Blueprint* and his highly informative web site on all things primal, Mark's Daily Apple.

CHRIS KRESSER For more in-depth science behind the paleo framework and nutrition in general, check out Chris Kresser's web site. His posts are lengthy, nerdy, and contain just the right dose of healthy skepticism.

PAUL JAMINET, PH.D. and **SHOU-CHING SHIH JAMINET, PH.D.** Paul, an astrophysicist and software entrepreneur, and his wife, Shou-Ching, a molecular biologist and cancer researcher, are the brains behind the *Perfect Health Diet* book and web site. The geek in me loves the information they provide and the cook in me loves that they approve of white rice and dairy foods.

CLAIRE YATES An Australian nutritional medicine practitioner and the founder of Indi Nature, a health and well-being blog, Claire is passionate about education and helping clients with digestive problems and emotional eating. Claire was one of the first practicing paleo nutritionists in Australia and is registered with the global evolutionary healthcare group, Primal Docs. I was fortunate enough to collaborate with Claire on Rejuvenate, a health and well-being program, which led to the creation of our joint web site, Rejuvenated For Life.

DIANE SANFILIPPO The founder of Balanced Bites and the author of *Practical Paleo*, Diane is another cool cat on the paleo streets. She is a sassy, classy, and smart holistic nutritionist specializing in paleo nutrition, blood-sugar regulation, food allergies and intolerances, and digestive health.

SALLY FALLON The co-founder of the Weston A. Price Foundation and author of *Nourishing Traditions*, a book every foodie and cook should read.

More resources and reading on the Eat Drink Paleo web site.

Paleo Basics

This cookbook won't give you all the hows and whys of the paleo diet. I believe there are much better books and resources on the science of paleo written by experienced evolutionary biologists, biochemists, nutritionists, and doctors. However, for those of you completely new to paleo, here is what you need to know.

♥ The paleo diet and lifestyle draw their core principles from our hunter-gatherer ancestors. It's not about re-enacting the Paleolithic era but rather recognizing our genetic predisposition and applying current scientific knowledge of how our diet and lifestyle choices affect our body and mind.

♥ The diet is based on nutrient-dense, whole, unprocessed ingredients, including lots of protein and healthful fats. It excludes pro-inflammatory, nutrient-void foods such as grains, processed sugars, and unhealthful vegetable and seed oils. The paleo lifestyle advocates stress management, sleep improvement, regular, primal-inspired exercise, and plenty of sunshine.

♥ People get into paleo for different reasons and experience different effects and changes in their bodies, mood, and energy levels as a result. Some of the reported and known benefits include improved metabolism and digestion, increased energy levels, sustained weight loss, improved sleep, mental clarity, clearer skin, a feeling of vitality, and overall well-being. You can read more about the benefits on my Eat Drink Paleo web site.

♥ There is no one-size-fits-all paleo diet. It's more a framework that can be tailored to individual needs, goals, body types, sensitivities, lifestyle, and budget. It's about nurturing your body and mind the best you can, and, most important, it's not just about the food.

The following foods get the paleo seal of approval. Depending on your health, lifestyle, and goals, some of these foods should be consumed in moderation. If you're trying to lose weight, improve your metabolism, or if you're suffering from insulin resistance or autoimmune-related diseases, intake of vegetables and non-grain flours high in carbohydrates and fruit high in sugar should be kept to a minimum. Some people need to avoid eggs, dairy, or nightshades, while others can enjoy them freely. Please consult your doctor or a qualified nutritionist on how to best adapt the paleo diet to your needs.

MEAT, SEAFOOD & EGGS

Includes beef, veal, lamb, pork, venison, game meats, bison, buffalo, goat, rabbit, chicken, duck, quail, pheasant, pigeon, goose, turkey, and organ meats such as liver, kidneys, and hearts, as well as chicken eggs and quail eggs.

Most fish, especially oily fish, shrimp, oysters, clams, mussels, snails, lobster, and crab.

♥ *Eat meat from grass-fed animals, butter from grass-fed cows, and free-range poultry and eggs. It's more nutritious and better for the planet and the animals.*

♥ *When buying sausages, look for gluten-free varieties with natural ingredients and as few additives and preservatives as possible.*

♥ *If you can't find any grass-fed meat in your local supermarket, try ordering online or directly from the farm.*

♥ *When buying fish and seafood, look for the most sustainable varieties available. Oily fish such as sardines, salmon, and trout are very high in omega-3 fatty acids and calcium, while shellfish is well known for its high content of minerals.*

What about deli meats?

If you're like me, you absolutely love cured meats such as salami, prosciutto, bacon, chorizo, and ham off the bone. Some paleo purists avoid cured meat, but there isn't much harm in consuming good-quality, naturally cured meats in moderation. Sure, they're salty, but we need some salt. They might contain nitrate or nitrite, but so do many other foods we eat, and, as Chris Kresser pointed out in his post on bacon, "There is no reason to fear nitrates and nitrites in food," especially the amounts present in cured meats. Bring on the bacon!

VEGETABLES

Most of the carbohydrates in the paleo diet come from stem and root vegetables and fruits. Your personal carbohydrate needs depend on your health and lifestyle. Mark Sisson, author of *The Primal Blueprint*, recommends consuming between 100 and 150 grams of carbohydrates per day for effortless weight maintenance, between 50 and 100 grams for moderate fat loss, and below 50 grams for accelerated fat loss. The intake can be higher for athletes and regular exercisers who need to replace post-workout glycogen stores.

Low carb (under 10 grams of carbohydrates per 100 grams)

Arugula, asparagus, avocados, bamboo shoots, bean sprouts, beet greens, bok choy, broccoli, Brussels sprouts, cabbage, cauliflower, cavolo nero, celery, chard, collard greens, cucumbers, daikon, dandelion greens, eggplant, endive, fennel, garlic, green beans, green onions, kale, kohlrabi, lettuce, mushrooms, mustard greens, okra, onions, peppers, pumpkin, radicchio, radishes, rhubarb, rutabaga, seaweed, shallots, snow peas, spinach, summer and spaghetti squash, tomatillos, tomatoes, turnips, turnip greens, watercress, zucchini, zucchini flowers.

Medium carb (10 to 20 grams of carbohydrates per 100 grams)

Artichokes, beets, butternut squash, carrots, green peas, Jerusalem artichokes, leeks, lotus root, parsnips.

High carb (more than 20 grams of carbohydrates per 100 grams)

Cassava (manioc), plantains, sweet potatoes, taro, white potatoes, winter squash, yams, yuccas.

♥ *Fresh is always best but frozen vegetables are still packed with nutrients and can be used freely if more convenient.*

♥ *Traditionally fermented vegetables are highly nutritious due to their probiotic properties.*

♥ *Depending on the ingredients and the preparation method, pickled vegetables can also retain most of their nutrients.*

♥ *Canned vegetables are usually precooked and contain very few nutrients by the time they get to your plate.*

♥ *When using white potatoes specifically, make sure to peel them to remove some of the anti-nutrients found in the skin.*

FRUITS & BERRIES

Low sugar (under 7 grams per 100 grams)

Avocados, black currants, blackberries, blueberries, boysenberries, cranberries, gooseberries, grapefruit, green mango, green papaya, huckleberries, lemon, lime, mulberries, papaya, raspberries, red currants, starfruit, strawberries.

Medium sugar (7 to 15 grams per 100 grams)

Apples, apricots, cantaloupe, cherries, fresh figs, guava, honeydew, kiwi fruit, oranges, passion fruit, peaches, pears, persimmons, plums, pomegranate, tangerines.

High sugar (more 15 grams per 100 grams)

Bananas, grapes, lychees, mangoes, nectarines, pineapple, plantains, watermelon.

FATS & OILS

The paleo diet embraces saturated fats and healthful plant-based oils, and avoids highly refined and processed polyunsaturated oils such as canola oil, vegetable oil, and margarine due to their toxic properties and high omega-6 fatty acids. Your fat intake should come from meat, seafood, eggs, nuts, avocados, and fats and oils used in food preparation. It's important to know which type of fat or oil is best suited to which food preparation method.

♥ *Saturated fat is typically more heat stable and doesn't oxidate as quickly as monounsaturated and polyunsaturated fats, which makes it more suitable for frying and other high-temperature cooking.*

♥ *Nut oils and olive oil are more fragile; they can be cooked with, but are best used unheated to retain the most antioxidants, vitamins, and flavor.*

♥ *Refined oils will usually have a higher smoking point. Ideally, they should be expeller-pressed, which indicates that the oil was extracted using a mechanical process rather than with heat and chemicals. These are best for high-temperature cooking such as deep-frying.*

OLIVE OIL

From highest to lowest temperature stability.

BEST FOR HOT USE	BEST FOR COLD USE
Lard, duck fat, tallow	Extra-virgin olive oil
Ghee	Macadamia oil
Macadamia oil	Avocado oil
Avocado oil	Sesame oil
Unrefined coconut oil	Hazelnut oil
Sesame oil	Almond or walnut oil
Olive oil	Flaxseed oil
Almond or walnut oil	Butter
Butter	Unrefined coconut oil

NUTS & SEEDS

Nuts and seeds are great for snacking and cooking with. However, along with lots of healthful fats, vitamins, and minerals, most nuts and seeds are high in pro-inflammatory omega-6 fatty acids and anti-nutrients such as phytic acid, which prevents mineral absorption in the body. This doesn't mean they're bad, but rather that you should try to learn about the nutritional content of different nuts and seeds and consume them in moderation. You should also soak nuts and seeds for 6 to 12 hours and then dehydrate them in sunlight, a dehydrator, or in an oven, which removes a high percentage of anti-nutrients. The table below shows the nuts and seeds that should be consumed least and in moderation based on their nutritional, fatty acids profile and anti-nutrients content.

BEST	IN MODERATION	SMALL AMOUNTS
Macadamia nuts	Almonds	Pumpkin seeds
Coconut, dried	Linseed	Walnuts
Chestnuts	Pistachios	Pine nuts
Hazelnuts	Cashews	Sunflower seeds
Flax seeds	Brazil nuts	Sesame seeds
Chia seeds	Pecans	

LIQUIDS

BEST

Water

Mineral water

Coconut milk and cream

Coconut water

Almond milk, fresh if possible

Herbal teas

Kefir (fermented dairy drink)

Kombucha (fermented tea)

Bone broth, natural meat and vegetable stocks

Vegetable juices

IN MODERATION

Black coffee, black tea

Low-sugar wine, sparkling wine, clear non-grain spirits such as vodka or tequila

Small amounts of freshly squeezed juices

DAIRY

Consumption of dairy is a contentious topic in paleo circles. Most agree that full-fat dairy, especially from grass-fed cattle, contains many essential nutrients and fats. However, dairy also contains lactose and casein protein, and is highly insulinogenic, which makes it problematic for people with metabolic and digestive issues. A common recommendation when transitioning to a paleo diet is to avoid all dairy for 30 days. After the elimination period, you can slowly reintroduce it and monitor if all or some dairy products cause any minor or major reactions in your body. If you feel better without, then it's best avoided.

I belong to the more relaxed paleo group and include select dairy products in my dishes. I avoid plain milk but I do love butter—which is almost all fat—a little full-fat yogurt, and aged cheeses. As with most foods, not all dairy is created equal. Raw, fermented, full-fat dairy is best, but it's not always easily accessible. I always look for organic, hormone- and antibiotic-free full-fat dairy from grass-fed animals. No fat-free yogurt, plastic cheese, or skim milk for me!

The following dairy products are considered more superior in a paleo diet based on their nutritional profile.

BEST

Ghee	Goat & sheep milk, cheese, and yogurt
Butter	Aged cheeses—Cheddar, Parmesan, pecorino
Kefir	Ricotta
Full-fat, unsweetened yogurt	Halloumi, especially from goat or sheep milk
Cream	Feta, especially from goat or sheep milk

ADD SOME FLAVOR

I use mostly fresh and dried herbs and spices, including lemongrass, lime leaves, garlic, ginger, galangal, turmeric, lavender, vanilla beans, and horseradish. I choose good-quality sea salt or Celtic salt for seasoning. I avoid spice mixtures and herbs that contain additives and preservatives. I blend my own instead.

I also use these common-place condiments in my paleo cooking—anchovies and anchovy paste; applesauce; capers; sun-dried tomatoes; gherkins; olives; tahini; coconut milk, coconut cream, and coconut butter; fish sauce; chili sauce; coconut aminos (similar to sweet soy sauce); most vinegars except for malt vinegar; mustard; truffles and truffle oil; dried wild mushrooms; tomato paste; and raw cacao, cocoa powder, and carob powder. When buying prepared pesto and sauces, I choose varieties with natural ingredients and avoid anything made with soybean, canola, or other vegetable oils and added sugar. Occasionally, I will use a wheat-free, gluten-free, naturally brewed soy sauce or tamari, but not very often.

SWEET THINGS

When necessary, I occasionally use natural sweeteners such as raw honey, pure maple syrup (grade B), molasses, dark chocolate, coconut syrup, coconut sugar, green-leaf stevia, applesauce, dates, prunes, dried apricots, dried figs, palm sugar, fresh fruit juices, raw sugar, and brown sugar.

WHAT ABOUT BAKING?

When it comes to baking, instead of all-purpose flour, try tapioca flour, chestnut flour, coconut flour, plantain flour, almond meal, hazelnut meal, macadamia meal, potato starch, gluten-free baking powder, baking soda, vegetable powders, ground nuts, and shredded or desiccated coconut. You can also use puréed fresh sweet potato, pumpkin, carrots, bananas, avocados, and other fruit, as well as eggs and coconut cream in baking.

what's out

The bad news is, you will have to say good-bye to foods that until now might have been on top of your shopping list. Don't worry, you'll never go hungry by giving up bread, beans, and pasta. You'll be surprised at the variety of meals you can prepare without the following ingredients.

GRAINS & LEGUMES

Despite a popular belief that grains, especially whole grains, are good for us, the paleo diet advocates a complete avoidance of grains, including wheat, barley, rice, and corn. Legumes are also avoided, as they share similar negative properties, outlined below.

♥ *Many grains contain gluten, a complex of proteins that can cause gut inflammation and damage to the gut lining, leading to malabsorption of nutrients. Gluten has also been associated with such conditions and symptoms as gastrointestinal issues, skin problems, autoimmune disease, and mental health issues.*

♥ *Grains and legumes are high in carbohydrates. The paleo diet is not against carbohydrates per se, but it does advocate a low-to-moderate intake, which is more suitable to modern lifestyles. Consuming more carbohydrates than your body needs can lead to problems such as insulin resistance, obesity, type 2 diabetes, and some cancers.*

♥ *Grains and legumes contain anti-nutrients—natural or synthetic compounds that inhibit the absorption of nutrients—such as phytic acid and lectins. Phytic acid, or phytates, is found in plant-based foods, most prevalently in grains and legumes and in moderate amounts in nuts and seeds. It prevents the absorption of some minerals into the bloodstream, and mineral deficiency has been linked to issues such as osteoporosis, skin conditions, muscle cramping, fatigue, infertility, poor immunity, and more. It's best to limit its consumption by avoiding grains and legumes and soaking nuts and seeds before use.*

♥ *Lectins are found in most plant-based foods and have especially high numbers in grains and legumes. Lectins are a naturally occurring defence mechanism in certain plants, which protect their survival by irritating the digestive system of the mammals consuming it, including us. Such damage to the gut lining impairs the absorption of nutrients.*

To play devil's advocate, I would like to point out that some ancient cultures consumed wild grains such as wild rice and corn. The difference between now and then is in the amounts consumed, the level of processing, and the cooking and preparation methods. The Weston A. Price Foundation dietary philosophy, based on studies of ancient cultures and their health, recommends fermentation, soaking, and a variety of cooking methods to improve the nutritional profile of certain grains and legumes and to remove some of the anti-nutrients.

Grains and legumes to avoid include, but are not limited to, the following.

GRAINS	LEGUMES	PSEUDOGRAINS
Wheat	Soybeans	Quinoa
Barley	Black-eyed peas	Amaranth
Rye	Red kidney beans	Chia seeds
Corn	Cannellini beans	Buckwheat
Spelt	Dal	Hemp
Bran	Split peas	Flax
Polenta	Lentils	
Millet	Chickpeas	
Oats	Lima beans	
Kamut	Borlotti beans	
Brown, wild, or white rice	Pinto beans	
Sorghum		

♥ *According to the Perfect Health Diet, white rice is essentially a carbohydrate with neither nutrients nor toxins, so although it's high in carbohydrates, it won't do much harm if consumed in small amounts.*

♥ *Legumes have to be soaked, fermented, or sprouted to make them safe to eat. For convenience, most choose to simply avoid them. Soybeans and soy products such as soy milk, tofu, and meat substitutes are most harmful and should be avoided, while some fermented soy foods, such as miso, natto, and naturally brewed wheat- and gluten-free soy sauce, can be eaten occasionally.*

♥ *"Pseudograins" contain anti-nutrient properties similar to grains and legumes; however, as they typically comprise more proteins, B vitamins, iron, and healthful fatty acids, they're considered more nutritious and safer to eat. Pseudograins can be consumed occasionally if handled properly by soaking and washing before cooking.*

PROCESSED, REFINED ARTIFICIAL SUGARS & SWEETENERS

I'm sure this is not the first time you've read that too much sugar is not good for you. The list of sugar "achievements" is long and well-documented: it's linked to overeating, hypoglycemia, obesity, diabetes, digestive problems, and the development of multiple cancers. But sweeteners aren't all bad. The nutritional value of sweeteners depends on how they're made, where they're used, and how our body processes them. Here is a roundup of sugars and sweeteners that should be avoided (including drinks and foods containing them).

Granulated white sugar, confectioners' sugar, high-fructose corn syrup, corn syrup, brown-rice malt syrup, malt syrup, beet sugar, barley malt, golden syrup, caramel, carob syrup, Demerara sugar, dextrose, fructose, grape sugar, maltose, maltodextrin, sorghum syrup, xylitol, light brown sugar, agave and agave nectar (90 percent fructose and only 10 percent glucose), aspartame (sold as NutraSweet or Equal), saccharin (Sweet'N Low), sucralose (Splenda), acesulfame K (Sunette or Sweet One), and sorbitol.

VEGETABLE & SEED OILS

While naturally occurring, minimally processed fats and oils (such as olive oil and butter) are a healthy source of energy and nutrients, highly processed vegetable and seed oils (such as soybean, canola, and corn oils) contain high levels of omega-6 fatty acids, which, when consumed in excess, have detrimental health effects. The problem is, these oils are present in nearly everything we eat nowadays. Grain-fed livestock, the source of the bulk of our meat supply, is also high in omega-6. A diet high in omega-6 is associated with an increase in inflammatory diseases such as cardiovascular disease, type 2 diabetes, rheumatoid arthritis, asthma, and cancer.

In addition to omega-6 fatty acids, most polyunsaturated oils are highly prone to oxidation and rancidity, which turns these so-called heart-healthy oils to toxic liquids. For these reasons, it's best to avoid corn, cottonseed, soybean, canola, safflower, sunflower, peanut, grapeseed, and vegetable oils, as well as margarine, which is made from the afore-mentioned oils.

A NOTE ON PROCESSED FOODS

Transitioning into paleo, I became very aware of how many processed foods—a.k.a. anything that comes in a package, bottle, or can—and by default, many restaurant meals, contain toxic ingredients such as gluten, processed sugars, and industrial oils. Much of the time you simply have to turn a blind eye on what oils and additives are used in meal preparation or you would have no social life. Depending on where you live, you can find products and brands that use mostly natural ingredients and ethical practices. For everything else, it's all about reading the labels. Cooking for yourself and your family gives you the ability to control what goes into your food.

And that's pretty much it, my friends. Before we get cooking, let me tell you what I have in my kitchen and refrigerator to create an easy paleo cooking experience.

KITCHEN BASICS

Little things

A few cutting boards, spatulas, can opener, colander, fine-mesh sieve, grater, handheld whisk, kettle, ladle, reamer, Mason jars, meat mallet, measuring cups, mortar and pestle, pastry brush, peeler, potato masher, rolling pin, tongs, salad spinner, slotted spoon, wooden spoon.

Dutch oven/casserole *Cook curries, roasts, braised meats, tagines, and soups. I use a large, heavy-lidded Le Creuset.*

Food processor *Chop, slice, grate, grind, blend, and purée in seconds.*

Blender *Purée and blend soups, smoothies, and condiments.*

Hand mixer *Whip, whisk, and blend; choose a five-speed model.*

Slow cooker *The ultimate magic pot! Cook large batches of braised meats, casseroles, tagines, and soups with minimum effort.*

Round cake pans/spring-form pan *Bake frittatas, sponge cakes, pies, and layered dishes.*

Loaf pan *Make banana bread, meatloaf, and terrines.*

Thermometer (dial or digital) *Check the doneness of roasted meats and measure liquid temperature.*

Grill or grill pan *Grill meats, seafood, and vegetables.*

Wok *Make quick stir-fries and fried cauliflower rice.*

Mandoline *Slice fruit and vegetables into really thin slices and ribbons.*

Juicer *Make vegetable juices to drink and to cook with.*

Airtight containers *Varied sizes of glass or steel containers with lids to store your kitchen prep and leftovers.*

Muffin pan *Use for egg muffins, cupcakes, and mini meat pies.*

Baking sheet [2] *Bake cookies, dehydrate nuts, make beef jerky, and oven-dry tomatoes.*

Roasting pan [2] *Use for roasting meats, vegetables, and baking lasagna, and large casseroles.*

Small saucepan *Boil eggs, make sauces, melt chocolate, heat soups.*

Medium saucepan *Make sauces, vegetables, and soups.*

Large saucepan *Cook large vegetables, simmer stocks, and sterilize jars.*

Small frying pan *Fry eggs and bacon, cook omelettes, sauté vegetables, thicken sauces.*

Large frying pan with high sides *Fry meat, sear roasts, and cook stews, vegetables, and meatballs.*

OPTIONAL: Fancy tools everyone raves about

Vitamix *Superhero appliance that can chop, beat, mix, cook, melt, emulsify, weigh, knead, and stir.*

Magic Bullet *A mini blender you can throw in your suitcase.*

Dehydrator *Dry out soaked nuts, make dried fruit and beef jerky.*

Bento-style lunch containers and a thermos *Take your meals on the go.*

in my pantry

I usually keep the following foods and ingredients in my pantry.
Many of these will move into the refrigerator after opening.

Dry goods
A collection of teas and coffee beans, almond meal, almonds, cashews, coconut flour, coconut syrup or coconut sugar, dark chocolate, gluten-free baking powder, macadamia nuts, natural stevia, pumpkin seeds, quinoa and white rice (for THOSE days), raw cacao powder, sesame seeds, tapioca flour, vanilla extract.

Liquids & condiments
Apple cider vinegar, balsamic vinegar, coconut aminos, coconut butter, coconut milk, coconut oil, coconut water, fish sauce, gluten-free Worcestershire sauce, hot sauce, macadamia oil, mustard, raw honey, red wine, sesame oil, tahini, olive oil, extra-virgin olive oil, white wine vinegar.

Spices & dried herbs
Basil, bay leaves, black pepper, cinnamon, cloves, coriander, cumin, curry powder, five-spice powder, garlic powder, nutmeg, oregano, paprika, parsley, red pepper flakes, rosemary, sea salt or Celtic salt, star anise, turmeric.

Jars & cans
Anchovies; artichokes; capers; gherkins; horseradish; pickled jalapeños; salmon; sardines; sun-dried tomatoes; crushed, diced, or whole tomatoes; tomato paste.

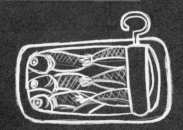

in my refrigerator

The inventory of fresh food in my house depends on the season and events, but on a typical day, after a big weekly shop, you will find the following in my refrigerator and on my countertop.

Fresh produce

Apples, avocados, bananas, bell peppers, berries, broccoli, cabbage, carrots, cauliflower, celery, cucumber, garlic, ginger, herbs, kiwi, lettuces, mushrooms, onions, pumpkin, radishes, spinach, sweet potatoes, tomatoes.

In the Freezer

Berries, green peas, sausages, soup, spinach, stock cubes.

Fats

Butter, ghee, fish oil.

Protein

Bacon, chicken, eggs, Greek-style yogurt or coconut yogurt, ground beef, halloumi, lamb chops or shanks, liver pâté, olives, Parmesan, salami, sauerkraut, shrimp.

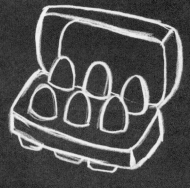

— my favorite —
blogs & web sites

♥ AUSTRALIA

Eat · Sleep · Move

Indi Nature

Lady Homemade

Modern Paleo

Nourishing Australia

Paleo Foodies

Paleo in Melbourne

Pete Evans

Rejuvenated For Life

Sarah Wilson

The Healthy Chef

The Merrymaker Sisters

The Paleo Network

What Katie Ate

♥ AROUND THE WORLD

Lookbook Cookbook

PaleoDish

Paleo Britain

Paleo Polly

Strictly Paleo...ish!

Swiss Paleo

The Fitness Explorer

♥ USA

Against All Grain

Balanced Bites

Cave Girl Eats

Chris Kresser

Civilized Caveman

Clothes Make The Girl

Elana's Pantry

Everyday Paleo

Living Paleo

Mark's Daily Apple

Nom Nom Paleo

Paleo Cupboard

PaleOMG

Paleo Parents

Primal Palate

Primal Toad

Robb Wolf

Rubies & Radishes

The Domestic Man

The Kitchn

The Paleo Mom

Wellness Mama

Weston A. Price

hazelnut pancakes with blood orange sauce

What better way to start a Sunday than sleeping in and making a batch of fluffy pancakes paired with freshly brewed coffee. These paleo pancakes have a slightly different texture, but people I've made them for prefer them to standard pancakes.

MAKES 12 PANCAKES

For the orange sauce

4 Tbsp butter

3 blood oranges; 1 juiced, 2 peeled and cut into slices

Juice from 1 navel orange

1 Tbsp lemon juice

2 tsp coconut sugar or raw honey

1 vanilla bean, halved lengthwise

For the pancakes

4 eggs

1 tsp vanilla extract

1 very ripe banana

2 Tbsp coconut flour

1½ cups ground hazelnuts

½ tsp baking soda or gluten-free baking powder

Ghee or coconut oil for frying

Whole toasted hazelnuts for garnish (optional)

To make the sauce: In a small saucepan over medium-high heat, melt the butter. Add the blood orange juice, navel orange juice, lemon juice, coconut sugar, and vanilla bean. Bring to a simmer, stirring, and add the slices of blood orange. Turn the heat to low and cook, stirring occasionally, for 15 minutes.

Meanwhile, to make the pancakes: In a medium bowl, whisk the eggs with the vanilla. Mash the banana and fold it into the egg mixture. Add the coconut flour and ground hazelnuts. Sprinkle the baking soda over all. Whisk until well combined.

In a large frying pan over medium heat, melt 1 tsp ghee. Spoon about ¼ cup of batter per pancake into the pan. Cook until bubbles appear on the surface, about 2 minutes. Flip, and cook for another minute. Transfer to a plate and cover loosely with aluminum foil to keep warm. Repeat with the remaining batter, brushing the pan with ghee as needed between batches. Serve warm, topped with the orange slices and drizzled with the sauce. Garnish with the whole hazelnuts, if you like.

If you don't have enough time to make the sauce, serve these pancakes with berries, banana, and some raw honey. If avoiding butter, add 2 Tbsp ghee or coconut oil to the sauce instead. Almond flour can be used instead of ground hazelnuts.

breakfast granola

We make this granola almost every week, as it's a perfect alternative to eggs and is also a great snack on the go. I usually have about ½ cup of granola with some yogurt and berries. Also try it with Homemade Coconut Yogurt (page 182).

MAKES 10 SERVINGS

Coconut oil for greasing

3 cups mixed almonds, hazelnuts, and macadamia nuts

⅔ cup dried plums, cherries, cranberries, or apricots, or a mixture

⅔ cup unsweetened shredded coconut

½ cup coconut flakes

½ cup pumpkin seeds

2 Tbsp maple syrup

2 to 3 Tbsp raw honey or coconut syrup

1 tsp vanilla extract

Zest of 1 orange (optional)

1 to 2 Tbsp chia seeds

Preheat the oven to 350°F. Grease a rimmed baking sheet with coconut oil and line with parchment paper.

Using a food processor, pulse 2½ cups of the nuts and all of the dried fruit into small crumbs.

In a large bowl, add the ground nut-fruit mixture, the remaining ½ cup whole nuts, the shredded coconut, coconut flakes, pumpkin seeds, maple syrup, honey, vanilla, and orange zest (if using). Stir with a wooden spoon until combined. Pour the mixture onto the prepared baking sheet and use a spatula to flatten it out.

Bake until browned, 20 to 25 minutes, stirring twice during the baking process. Remove to a wire rack and let cool completely. Stir in the chia seeds. Store in an airtight container at room temperature for up to 2 weeks.

asparagus soldiers, eggs & truffle

Ever since I was a little girl, I've loved eggs and soldiers. These days, since I don't eat bread, I use whatever else I can find to dip into a creamy, nutritious egg yolk. Using asparagus sautéed in some butter and truffle oil takes the experience to the next level.

SERVES 2

4 eggs, at room temperature

1 tsp butter or olive oil

1 tsp truffle oil

12 asparagus spears, ends trimmed

Sea salt and freshly ground black pepper

Bring a small saucepan with enough water to cover the eggs to a boil, then remove from the heat. Using a slotted spoon, gently lower the eggs into the hot water. Let the eggs settle for 10 seconds, then place the saucepan over high heat to bring the water back to a boil. Cook for 5 minutes for a soft center and firm whites. Run the hot eggs under cold water for 15 seconds to stop the cooking and to make peeling them easier.

In a small frying pan over medium heat, melt the butter with the truffle oil. Add the asparagus and cook for 1 to 2 minutes, turning often, until crisp-tender. Sprinkle with a little sea salt and pepper and serve immediately, with the eggs.

Truffle-infused oil is usually made with extra-virgin olive oil that's been infused with truffles. Invest in a small bottle from a gourmet shop and it will last you for ages. Add to scrambled eggs, mashed cauliflower, roasted mushrooms, steak sauces, and salad dressings.

velvet summer quiche

"Velvet summer" is that period when summer crosses into autumn, when the nights get cold but during the day the sun is still warm and feels like velvet on your skin. It's the time you get back into comfort food and baking. The flavors and texture of this quiche remind me of that gorgeous time of year.

SERVES 4 TO 6

4 tsp coconut oil or ghee

1 sweet potato, peeled and diced

2 yellow onions, sliced

1 red bell pepper, seeded and sliced

2 Tbsp thyme leaves, plus more for sprinkling

5 garlic cloves, minced

1 Tbsp balsamic vinegar

Sea salt

10 eggs

⅔ cup heavy cream (optional)

Zest of 1 lemon

Freshly ground black pepper

½ cup grated Parmesan or cheddar cheese

⅓ cup pine nuts

Preheat the oven to 400°F. Grease a baking sheet with 1 tsp of the coconut oil. Spread the sweet potato on the prepared sheet. Bake for 20 minutes, or until tender. Remove from the oven and set aside. Lower the oven temperature to 350°F.

In a medium frying pan over medium heat, melt 2 tsp coconut oil. Add the onions and bell pepper and cook for about 15 minutes, or until tender. After 10 minutes, add the thyme, garlic, vinegar, and a pinch of salt.

In a small bowl, whisk the eggs with the cream (if using). Add the lemon zest, a pinch of salt, a pinch of black pepper, and the Parmesan.

Grease a rimmed baking sheet with the remaining 1 tsp coconut oil and line with parchment paper. Layer the sweet potato and then the onion mixture evenly on the parchment. Pour the egg mixture over the vegetables. Bake for 10 minutes. Sprinkle the pine nuts and more fresh thyme over all and bake for 15 minutes more. Let cool for 5 minutes.

Lift the quiche from the pan using the parchment. Transfer to a cutting board, slice, and serve warm.

> You can also use a round baking pan or springform. If avoiding dairy, prepare without the cream and cheese; the quiche will lack the creaminess and fluffy texture. Store, refrigerated, for up to 4 days.

banana bread

This banana bread is super easy to make and tastes just as good as a wheat-flour version. I make this a lot, as it's very handy to have a few slices around for snacks, lunches, travel, and breakfast on the go.

SERVES 10

Coconut oil for brushing, plus
2½ Tbsp

3 eggs

Pinch of sea salt

2 very ripe bananas, mashed

1 Tbsp raw honey or maple syrup

1 tsp vanilla extract

1½ cups almond flour

3 Tbsp tapioca flour

2 Tbsp unsweetened shredded coconut

1 tsp gluten-free baking powder

1 tsp ground cinnamon

Pinch of freshly grated nutmeg

3 Tbsp chopped walnuts, plus more for topping

¼ cup diced dried apricots or figs

Butter for serving (optional)

Preheat the oven to 350°F. Brush a loaf pan with coconut oil and line the bottom with parchment paper.

Method 1: In a large mixing bowl, whisk the eggs and salt until thick and foamy. Add the bananas, honey, vanilla, and 2½ Tbsp coconut oil. Whisk until well incorporated. Add the almond flour, tapioca, shredded coconut, baking powder, cinnamon, and nutmeg and stir to combine. Fold in the walnuts and dried apricots.

Method 2: Place the eggs, salt, bananas, honey, vanilla, and 2½ Tbsp coconut oil in a blender. Process for 20 to 30 seconds, until thick and foamy. Add the almond flour, tapioca, shredded coconut, baking powder, cinnamon, and nutmeg. Blend until smooth and thick, stopping to scrape down the sides of the jar once or twice. Fold in the walnuts and dried apricots.

Pour the batter into the prepared pan. Smooth the surface and arrange a few walnuts on top.

Bake for 45 to 55 minutes. Insert a bamboo skewer or toothpick into the center of the bread; if it comes out dry, it's done. Let cool for 5 to 10 minutes on a wire rack before turning it out of the pan. Cover with a towel if cooling overnight. Serve warm or at room temperature, as is or toasted and smothered with butter.

harissa-chorizo egg crepes

This recipe was a bit of an accident. It's a mash-up of a savory crepe and a Mexican breakfast burrito. Luckily, it was so delicious it made it into this cookbook.

SERVES 2

2 Tbsp olive oil

½ yellow onion, diced

½ red bell pepper, seeded and diced

4 oz Spanish chorizo

1 Tbsp Lemony Harissa (page 176)

6 eggs

Pinch of sea salt

1 tsp ghee

Cilantro leaves for serving

Avocado slices for serving

In a small frying pan over medium heat, warm the olive oil. Sauté the onion and bell pepper for 3 to 4 minutes, until softened.

Meanwhile, peel the chorizo, cut it into chunks, and mince. Add it to the pan with the onion and bell pepper. Add the harissa, stir, and cook until the meat is browned and slightly caramelized, 3 to 4 minutes. Remove from the heat and set aside.

In a small bowl, whisk the eggs with the salt.

In a medium frying pan over medium heat, warm ½ tsp of the ghee for 30 seconds. Ladle in just enough of the egg mixture to coat the bottom of the pan. Swirl the egg around in the pan to form a thin pancake. Cook for 1 minute. Run a spatula around the outside edges of the crepe as it cooks to loosen it. Gently lift and flip (you might not even need to if it's thin enough to cook through from the bottom). Cook the second side for 15 seconds. Slide onto a plate and repeat with the remaining ghee and egg mixture.

Place half of the chorizo mixture in the center of each crepe. Fold into thirds like an envelope and serve garnished with cilantro and avocado.

> Chorizo is a smoked Spanish sausage made with pork and lots of paprika, garlic, and other spices. Look for good-quality chorizo made with natural ingredients. Harissa is a spicy North African chile sauce. Make it yourself, or use a good-quality purchased harissa.

chai banana porridge

Warm and nourishing, this porridge is a treat that tastes like something you might be served while on a yoga retreat in India. Save it for the weekend, when you have time to enjoy it slowly.

SERVES 2

½ cup macadamia nuts

½ cup almonds

1 very ripe banana, plus banana slices for garnish

1 cup coconut milk

½ cup water

½ cup unsweetened shredded coconut

1 Tbsp chia seeds

1 tsp vanilla extract

½ tsp ground cardamom

½ tsp ground ginger

½ tsp ground cinnamon, plus more for sprinkling

Pinch of freshly gratred nutmeg

Pinch of sea salt

1 Tbsp raw honey

Fresh berries for topping

In a food processor, pulse the macadamia nuts and almonds into small crumbs; be careful not to overgrind or they will turn into nut butter. Add the banana and process just until the banana is puréed. (Alternatively, you can use a fork to mash the banana and a mortar and pestle to pulverize the nuts.) Transfer the mixture to a small saucepan.

Place the pan over medium heat and add the coconut milk, water, shredded coconut, chia seeds, vanilla, cardamom, ginger, cinnamon, nutmeg, and salt. Bring to a simmer and cook, stirring, until soft, 3 to 4 minutes. Serve immediately, drizzled with the honey, topped with berries and sliced banana, and sprinkled with cinnamon.

To speed up the process, you can keep a larger batch of processed nuts mixed with spices in a jar in the pantry, ready to go, for up to 1 month.

zucchini & bacon fritters

Fancy a little café breakfast at home? You can't go wrong with tasty, filling fritters. Make a bigger batch and have some for the next day's lunch and snacks. Kids love these, too.

SERVES 3

For the onion relish

3 Tbsp extra-virgin olive oil

2 yellow onions, sliced

1 red jalapeño, seeded and diced

½ tsp sea salt

1 garlic clove, minced

2 Tbsp balsamic vinegar

1 Tbsp tomato paste

½ tsp ground coriander

½ cup water

For the fritters

2 slices bacon, trimmed of excess fat and diced

Ghee for frying (optional)

2 zucchini, grated (do not use the seedy center)

1 carrot, grated

½ cup chopped green onions, plus more for garnish

2 eggs

2 Tbsp tapioca flour

½ tsp sea salt

½ tsp freshly ground black pepper

¼ tsp gluten-free baking powder

3 Tbsp coconut oil

To make the relish: In a medium frying pan over medium-high heat, warm the olive oil. Add the onions, jalapeño, and salt and turn the heat to medium-low. Sauté for about 5 minutes. Add the garlic, vinegar, tomato paste, coriander, and water. Stir and cook until softened and caramelized, about 15 minutes. Set aside and cover to keep warm.

To make the fritters: In another medium frying pan over medium heat, cook the bacon until crispy, adding a bit of ghee if necessary. Transfer to a paper towel–lined plate to drain.

In a large bowl, combine the bacon, zucchini, carrot, green onions, eggs, tapioca, salt, pepper, and baking powder and stir into a thick, moist batter. In a large frying pan over medium-high heat, warm the coconut oil. Using a large serving spoon, scoop the batter mixture and gently place in the hot oil, spacing them about ½ inch apart. Fry until a golden brown crust forms on the first side, about 3 minutes. Flip and cook on the second side until golden, about 3 minutes longer (adding more coconut oil if needed). Serve warm with the onion relish, garnished with green onions.

Tapioca flour can be replaced with almond flour, chestnut flour, or potato starch. Coconut flour can also be used but it will absorb more liquid, which might result in slightly drier fritters. If avoiding nightshades, remove the jalapeño from the relish recipe and replace with some ground black or white pepper for heat. You can use the leftover onion relish with grilled lamb, or fold it into a frittata. Leftover zucchini and carrot peel can be used for a master vegetable stock.

sweet potato rosti with sardine salad

Paleo breakfasts are not just about eggs. Whenever I feel I need a little break from omelettes, I turn to this other savory favorite. This dish packs a lot of energy, vitamin C, beta-carotene, and omega-3 fatty acids.

SERVES 2

2 Tbsp coconut oil or ghee

1 medium sweet potato, peeled and grated

½ tsp sea salt

½ tsp freshly ground black pepper

½ cucumber, peeled and sliced

1 cup sliced fennel bulb

½ green apple, thinly sliced

½ red onion, thinly sliced

1 Tbsp chopped dill

1 Tbsp extra-virgin olive oil

1 Tbsp lemon juice

10 sardine fillets, drained

1 Tbsp mayonnaise

In a medium frying pan over medium-high heat, melt the coconut oil until sizzling hot. Add the grated sweet potato, spread in an even layer, and flatten with a spatula. Turn the heat to medium and cook, scraping and turning every couple of minutes, for a total of 10 minutes. Stir in the sea salt and pepper. Remove the rosti from the heat and set aside.

In a medium bowl, toss together the cucumber, fennel, apple, onion and dill. Drizzle in the olive oil and lemon juice and toss to coat.

Divide the sardines among salad plates. Mound the salad on top of the sardine fillets and serve with a side of sweet potato rosti and a dollop of the mayonnaise.

> Use mayonnaise made with olive oil or macadamia oil rather than the standard soybean- or vegetable oil–based varieties. Try the recipe for homemade mayo on page 191. Canned salmon or tuna can be used instead of sardines.

macadamia & artichoke stuffed mushrooms

Here is another egg-free recipe to add to your breakfast repertoire. The mushrooms can be stuffed the night before, so all you have to do in the morning is stick them in the oven while you're getting ready.

In a bowl, soak the macadamia nuts in water to cover for 3 to 4 hours.

In a medium frying pan over medium heat, melt 1 Tbsp of the ghee. Add the onion and sauté until soft and golden. Remove from the heat and set aside.

Drain the nuts and place in a food processor with the artichokes, cooked onion, garlic, lemon zest, salt, pepper, and 1 Tbsp ghee. Process to a smooth, thick paste.

Preheat the oven to 350°F and grease a baking sheet with the remaining 1 Tbsp ghee. Fill each mushroom with about 1 tsp of the macadamia-artichoke mixture. Place on the prepared baking sheet and bake for 20 to 30 minutes.

Serve warm, garnished with the parsley and crispy bacon.

You could use 4 to 6 larger portobello mushrooms instead of smaller button mushrooms. Cashew nuts can be used instead of macadamia nuts. If you eat butter, add that to the filling instead of ghee or olive oil for richer flavor.

SERVES 2

½ cup macadamia nuts

3 Tbsp ghee or olive oil

1 yellow onion, diced

⅔ cup canned artichokes, drained

1 garlic clove

Zest from 1 lemon

½ tsp sea salt

Pinch of freshly ground black pepper

12 large button mushrooms, brushed clean and stemmed

Parsley leaves for serving

Crispy-cooked bacon, crumbled

smoked salmon "not bagel"

I've always been a big fan of bagels with smoked salmon but, since I don't eat bagels anymore, I've decided to create a bagel-like sandwich using sweet potato patties. This recipe is very simple, and the final result is a worthy substitute that satisfies my smoked salmon bagel cravings.

SERVES 1

1 medium sweet potato, peeled and grated

1 Tbsp coconut flour

A few pinches of sea salt

Pinch of freshly ground black pepper

1 Tbsp ghee or coconut oil

1 Tbsp mayonnaise

2 or 3 slices smoked salmon

¼ red onion, thinly sliced

1 Tbsp capers, drained

Baby arugula or spinach leaves for serving (optional)

In a medium bowl, combine the sweet potato, coconut flour, salt, and pepper. Stir until a sticky dough forms.

In a medium frying pan over medium heat, melt the ghee. Using your hands, mold the potato mixture into two fat, round patties and place in the hot pan. Flatten with a spatula and cook until nicely browned on the first side, about 5 minutes. Flip and cook until golden on the second side and hot throughout, about 5 minutes longer.

Serve warm with a dollop of mayo on each patty and the smoked salmon, red onion, and capers sandwiched in between. Add some baby arugula or spinach leaves, if you like.

superstar egg muffins

Full disclosure: This is not my recipe! Yes, I've made something similar but not this particular combination. It is actually my boyfriend's creation, and I have his permission to use it in this cookbook because it's a favorite at home. Everyone absolutely loves these easy, tasty muffins.

SERVES 3

1 to 2 Tbsp extra-virgin olive oil

1 yellow onion, diced

5 slices salami or chorizo sausage, diced

4 thick slices halloumi cheese

6 eggs

Pinch of sea salt

Pinch of freshly ground black pepper

Avocado slices, cherry tomatoes, sauerkraut, and/or chili sauce for serving (optional)

Preheat the oven to 350°F. Lightly grease the wells of a muffin pan.

In a small frying pan over medium heat, warm the olive oil. Add the onion and cook until soft and golden, about 5 minutes. Transfer to a plate. Add the salami to the pan and cook until browned and crispy, about 5 minutes. Transfer to the plate with the onion. Add the halloumi slices to the pan and cook until they form a golden brown crust, about 1 minute on each side. Transfer the halloumi to a cutting board and cut into small pieces. Add to the plate with the salami-onion mixture and set aside.

In a medium bowl, whisk the eggs with the salt and pepper. Divide the salami-onion mixture among the prepared muffin wells. Make sure you have an even amount of all three ingredients in each. Pour the egg mixture into the wells, dividing it evenly. Carefully transfer the pan to the oven and bake until the egg muffins have risen and firmed up, about 17 minutes.

The muffins will fall but hold their shape once you remove them from the oven. Serve warm with sides of avocado, cherry tomatoes, sauerkraut, and chili sauce, as you like.

Halloumi cheese is a salty, semihard cheese, traditionally made with goat's and/or sheep's milk, and sometimes with cow's milk. We precook the cheese, onion, and salami mixture the night before to save time in the morning. You can omit the cheese and use other combinations such as sun-dried tomatoes and mushrooms or cooked spinach.

asparagus with warm mushroom dressing

SERVES 2 OR 3

½ cup dried porcini mushrooms

¼ cup olive oil or macadamia oil

½ yellow onion, diced

7 button mushrooms, brushed clean and diced

1 garlic clove, minced

1 Tbsp white wine vinegar

½ tsp sea salt

½ tsp freshly ground black pepper

1 tsp coconut oil or ghee

2 bunches asparagus stems, ends trimmed

Truffle oil for drizzling

Parsley leaves for sprinkling

In a small bowl, cover the porcini mushrooms with about 1 inch of water. Soak until soft, 15 to 30 minutes. Drain and chop.

In a medium frying pan over medium heat, warm the olive oil. Add the onion and sauté until soft, about 5 minutes. Add the chopped porcini and the button mushrooms. Cook for 3 to 4 minutes longer. Stir in the garlic, vinegar, salt, and pepper. Cook for a few minutes longer. Set aside and cover to keep warm.

In a large frying pan over medium-high heat, melt the coconut oil. Add the asparagus and cook just to brown, about 1 minute on each side. Arrange on a platter and pour the warm mushrooms over all. Drizzle with truffle oil and sprinkle parsley leaves on top. Serve warm or at room temperature.

You can use this mushroom dressing on other grilled vegetables or serve it on top of chicken or steak. Dried porcini mushrooms can be purchased from most good grocery stores. Use leftover dried porcini in a sweet potato shepherd's pie, a mushroom soup, or sauces.

lemongrass-pumpkin soup

This is one of the best pumpkin soups I've ever had. No kidding! It's really tasty and easy to prepare.

SERVES 2

2 tsp coconut oil

1 yellow onion, diced

1 stalk lemongrass, cut into thirds

1 red jalapeño, seeded; ½ diced, ½ sliced

2 Tbsp chopped cilantro stems, plus cilantro leaves for serving

One ¾-inch piece galangal

One ¾-inch piece turmeric root

4 lime leaves (optional)

3 cups peeled and cubed pumpkin

1 garlic clove, minced

Zest from ½ lime, cut into large strips, plus 2 Tbsp lime juice

2 Tbsp fish sauce

1 qt vegetable stock

½ cup coconut cream, plus more for garnish

In a large saucepan over medium-high heat, melt the coconut oil. Add the onion, lemongrass, diced jalapeño, cilantro stems, galangal, turmeric, and lime leaves (if using) and sauté for 2 to 3 minutes. Add the cubed pumpkin, garlic, lime zest, fish sauce, and vegetable stock and bring to boil. Turn the heat to medium-low and simmer, covered, until the pumpkin is tender when tested with a knife, about 15 minutes.

Remove from the heat and let cool slightly. Remove the turmeric, galangal, lime zest, lime leaves, and lemongrass from the soup and discard. Transfer the soup to a food processor or blender. Purée until smooth, in batches if necessary. Add the coconut cream and lime juice and process a couple more times to incorporate.

Return the soup to the pan and reheat gently. Serve with a ripple of coconut cream and a sprinkling of sliced jalapeño and cilantro leaves on top.

The fresh roots can be replaced with ½ tsp turmeric powder and ½ tsp galangal powder. Red kuri or butternut squash can be used in place of the pumpkin; sweet potato and carrots also work well. Coconut milk can be used instead of coconut cream, but refrigerate the can for about an hour before use to thicken the top half of the liquid.

smoked chicken slaw

Both traditional coleslaw and a Ukrainian salad called dnestr, made with the local sliced salami and tinned peas, inspire this salad. It's very versatile—you can make it for lunch or dinner, take it to picnics and barbecues, or divide it into batches for quick and easy lunches.

SERVES 6

½ **small green cabbage, cored and shredded**

2 **medium carrots, shredded**

2 **smoked chicken breasts, thinly sliced**

½ **cup green peas**

1 **small red onion, thinly sliced**

2 **Tbsp chopped fresh dill**

¼ **cup mayonnaise**

1 **Tbsp extra-virgin olive oil**

3 **Tbsp white wine vinegar**

½ **tsp sea salt**

½ **tsp freshly ground black pepper**

In a large bowl, toss together the cabbage, carrots, chicken, peas, onion, and dill.

In a small bowl, whisk together the mayonnaise, olive oil, vinegar, salt, and pepper until well incorporated.

Combine the salad and the dressing 10 minutes before serving and toss to coat well.

Good-quality sliced ham or cooked chicken can be used instead of smoked chicken. Try to use a mayonnaise made with olive or macadamia oil; see the recipe on page 191. If you plan to store some of the salad as leftovers, don't add the dressing until you're ready to eat it. This will keep the salad fresh and crispy for a few days.

kale-avocado gazpacho

Inspired by traditional tomato gazpacho, this refreshing green soup (pictured opposite) is like an IV full of antioxidants and healthful fats.

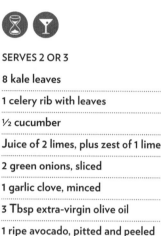

SERVES 2 OR 3

8 kale leaves

1 celery rib with leaves

½ cucumber

Juice of 2 limes, plus zest of 1 lime

2 green onions, sliced

1 garlic clove, minced

3 Tbsp extra-virgin olive oil

1 ripe avocado, pitted and peeled

Sea salt and freshly ground black pepper

Parsley or basil leaves for garnish

Juice the kale and celery; you should get about ½ cup dark green juice. Transfer to a blender. Peel and chop the cucumber and add to the blender along with the lime juice, 1 cup water, green onions, garlic, olive oil, avocado, ½ tsp salt, and ½ tsp pepper.

Process until smooth. Refrigerate for about 10 minutes. Serve in small bowls or chilled glasses. Garnish with the lime zest, parsley leaves, and a sprinkling of black pepper.

simple roasted pepper gazpacho

SERVES 2

2 red bell peppers

Coconut oil for rubbing

4 medium tomatoes

2 garlic cloves, minced

½ red onion, diced

1 cucumber, peeled and diced

⅓ cup extra-virgin olive oil

Juice of ½ lemon

1 tsp balsamic vinegar

Sea salt and freshly ground black pepper

Preheat the oven to 400°F. Line a baking sheet with aluminum foil. Rub the bell peppers with coconut oil and place on the prepared sheet. Roast until soft and charred, about 50 minutes, turning after 25 minutes. Let cool.

Meanwhile, bring a saucepan of water to a boil. Gently drop in the tomatoes and cook for 30 seconds. Drain, rinse under cold water, peel off the skins, and roughly chop. Set aside.

Peel and seed the cooled peppers. Transfer to a blender or food processor. Add the tomatoes, garlic, onion, cucumber, olive oil, 1½ cups water, lemon juice, and vinegar; season with salt and pepper; and purée until smooth. Refrigerate for about 10 minutes before serving.

mash three ways

I grew up on mashed potatoes, with my grandmother's amazing meatballs, marinated tomatoes, or a herring salad. Enjoy these paleo-friendly sides with your favorite roast meat or grilled fish. Use leftovers for a pie crust or as a side with your eggs in the morning.

SWEET POTATO–BACON MASH

MAKES 3 CUPS

1 sweet potato, peeled and cubed

2 Tbsp ghee

2 slices bacon, diced

¼ cup almond milk

½ tsp sea salt

½ tsp freshly ground black pepper

½ tsp Dijon mustard

1 Tbsp grated Parmesan cheese (optional)

In a medium saucepan, cover the sweet potato with cold water. Bring to a boil over medium-high heat and cook until tender when tested with a knife, about 15 minutes. Drain and set aside.

In a small frying pan over medium heat, melt 1 Tbsp of the ghee. Add the bacon and cook until crispy. Transfer the bacon to a plate and pour the drippings from the frying pan into the pan with the cooked sweet potato. Add the remaining 1 Tbsp ghee, the almond milk, salt, pepper, and mustard. Mash (or purée in a food processor) until smooth. Add the cheese, if you like. Fold in the bacon and serve.

BROCCOLI & RICOTTA MASH

MAKES 3 CUPS

1 potato, peeled and cubed

1 small head broccoli, broken into florets

2 Tbsp ricotta cheese

Zest of 1 lemon, plus 1 Tbsp lemon juice

1 Tbsp olive oil

½ tsp sea salt

Pinch of freshly ground black pepper

Parsley or mint leaves for garnish

In a medium saucepan, cover the potato with cold water. Bring to boil over medium-high heat and cook for 10 minutes, then add the broccoli and cook until both vegetables are soft, about 5 minutes longer. Drain and transfer the potato and broccoli to a food processor. Add the ricotta, lemon zest, lemon juice, olive oil, salt, and pepper. Process until smooth. Garnish with fresh parsley and serve.

Continued

BROCCOLi

SWEET POTATO

cauliflower

——— mash three ways continued ———

CAULIFLOWER-SAGE BUTTER MASH

MAKES 3 CUPS

½ head cauliflower, broken into florets

3 Tbsp butter

Handful of sage leaves

2 garlic cloves, sliced

Sea salt

½ cup almond milk or vegetable stock

Freshly ground black pepper

1 recipe Smoky Oyster Mushrooms (page 164)

Bring a medium saucepan of water to a boil over medium-high heat. Add the cauliflower and cook until very soft, about 15 minutes. Drain and transfer to a food processor.

Meanwhile, in a large frying pan over medium heat, melt the butter. Add the sage, garlic, and a pinch of salt. Cook, stirring, until the butter foams and turns golden and the sage leaves get crispy. Transfer the sage leaves to a paper towel to drain and add the melted butter to the food processor. Add the almond milk and purée into smooth mash. Season with salt and pepper. Serve topped with the crispy sage leaves and smoky mushrooms.

———baked parsnips with sage———

SERVES 2

10 parsnips, peeled and halved lengthwise

3 Tbsp ghee, melted

15 sage leaves

Zest of 1 lemon, cut into large strips, plus 2 Tbsp lemon juice

3 garlic cloves, thinly sliced

Sea salt

Preheat the oven to 350°F. On a baking sheet, toss the parsnips in the melted ghee. Spread in a single layer on the baking sheet and roast for 10 minutes. Add the sage leaves, lemon zest, and garlic and toss to mix. Roast until the parsnips are tender, about 15 minutes longer. Sprinkle with salt and drizzle with lemon juice before serving.

cauliflower steaks with wilted radicchio

SERVES 2

1 tsp coconut oil

1 medium cauliflower, cut into ¾-inch-thick steaks

Sea salt and freshly ground black pepper

1 Tbsp ghee

3 shallots, thinly sliced

2 garlic cloves, minced

1 Tbsp white wine vinegar

1 cup shredded radicchio

Handful of watercress sprigs or baby spinach leaves

1 Tbsp extra-virgin olive oil

Lemon wedges for serving

Preheat the oven to 400°F. In a large frying pan over medium-high heat, melt the coconut oil until sizzling hot. Add the cauliflower steaks and cook until golden brown, about 2 minutes per side. Season with salt and pepper and transfer to a baking sheet. Bake until tender, about 15 minutes.

Meanwhile, in a medium frying pan over medium heat, melt the ghee. Add the shallots and sauté for 5 minutes. Add the garlic, vinegar, ½ tsp salt, and ½ tsp pepper and cook for 2 to 3 minutes longer. Add the shredded radicchio, stir, and cook until slightly wilted, 1 to 2 minutes.

Top the cauliflower steaks with the radicchio and the watercress, drizzle with the olive oil, and serve with lemon wedges.

Use leftover cauliflower florets for roasting (see recipe on page 162) or in cauliflower fritters.

zucchini carbonara

Contrary to the popular belief that the creaminess of a carbonara comes from cream, it's actually the lightly cooked eggs and melted Parmesan cheese that coat the pasta. Using zucchini instead of pasta creates a guilt-free version (pictured opposite) of the classic. Lemon zest adds a little freshness. Those avoiding all dairy can use a couple of tablespoons of nutritional yeast instead of Parmesan cheese.

SERVES 2

1 tsp ghee or macadamia oil

4 slices bacon, diced

1 Tbsp extra-virgin olive oil

1 garlic clove, minced

4 zucchini, thinly sliced lengthwise

1 tsp lemon zest

½ tsp sea salt

½ tsp freshly ground black pepper

2 eggs, beaten

2 Tbsp grated Parmesan cheese

In a medium frying pan over medium-high heat, melt the ghee until sizzling hot. Add the bacon and cook until crispy.

Turn the heat to medium. Add the olive oil and garlic and sauté for 2 minutes. Add the zucchini, lemon zest, salt, and pepper and stir well. Cook for about 1 minute, then add the eggs. Stir constantly until the zucchini is well coated and the egg starts to cook and thicken, 1 to 2 minutes. Don't overcook the zucchini; it's all about the crunch. Remove from the heat, fold in the Parmesan, and serve.

asian sesame-cucumber salad

SERVES 4

1 tsp ghee

5 shiitake mushroom caps, sliced

4 Lebanese cucumbers, thinly shaved or sliced

2 Tbsp extra-virgin olive oil

2 Tbsp lime juice

1 tsp fish sauce

1 tsp sesame oil

1 Tbsp coconut aminos

2 Tbsp white or black sesame seeds

In a medium frying pan over medium heat, melt the ghee. Add the mushrooms and sauté until lightly browned on both sides, 3 to 4 minutes. Transfer to a bowl. Add the sliced cucumbers to the bowl with the mushrooms.

In a small bowl, whisk together the olive oil, lime juice, fish sauce, sesame oil, and coconut aminos. Pour over the cucumbers and mushrooms, toss with the sesame seeds, and serve immediately.

tuscan cabbage

Also known as cavolo nero, Tuscan cabbage is another green leafy vegetable to add to your cooking repertoire. It has narrow, wrinkled, dark green leaves and a mild flavor, similar to kale. It's great in soups and salads, but I love it sautéed and combined with punchy flavors.

SERVES 2

¼ cup macadamia nuts

8 sun-dried tomatoes, chopped

2 garlic cloves, chopped

1 Tbsp lemon zest, plus juice of ¼ lemon

4 Tbsp extra-virgin olive oil

1 bunch Tuscan cabbage, cut into shreds

½ cup white wine vinegar

1 Tbsp butter or ghee

½ tsp sea salt

Pinch of freshly ground black pepper

In a food processor, combine the macadamia nuts, sun-dried tomatoes, garlic, lemon zest, and 2 Tbsp of the olive oil and process into a crumbly mixture.

In a large frying pan over medium heat, warm the remaining 2 Tbsp olive oil. Add the nut mixture and cook until fragrant and the garlic is slightly golden brown, 3 to 4 minutes. Add the cabbage and vinegar and cook, stirring, for 5 minutes. Add the butter, salt, and pepper and cook for 5 minutes longer. Drizzle with the lemon juice just before serving.

This dish can be served with eggs for breakfast or with fish or meat for lunch and dinner. Similar to kale, Tuscan cabbage can also be made into chips or juiced to make green power smoothies.

ratatouille cake

Well before it was made famous by a certain cartoon rat, a hearty ratatouille was a regular vegetable dish at our home. This particular recipe is a ratatouille on steroids, with even more vegetable goodness and flavor packed into a grand-looking layered cake.

SERVES 8

3 large eggplants, cut lengthwise into slices about ½ inch thick

4 Tbsp extra-virgin olive oil

2 large zucchini, cut lengthwise into slices about ¼ inch thick

2 red bell peppers, seeded and cut into wide strips

Sea salt

3 Tbsp tomato paste

2 Tbsp thyme leaves, plus small sprigs for garnish

2 garlic cloves, minced

Freshly ground black pepper

Prepare a gas or charcoal grill to medium-high. Preheat the oven to 400°F. Line an 8-inch cake pan with aluminum foil and line the foil with parchment paper.

Brush the eggplant slices with 3 Tbsp of the olive oil. Arrange the eggplant on the grill rack, cover, and cook until nicely grill marked and the eggplant softens, 2 to 3 minutes per side. Transfer to a plate and set aside.

In a bowl, toss the zucchini and bell pepper slices with the remaining 1 Tbsp olive oil and a few pinches of salt. Arrange on the grill rack and cook for a few minutes on each side. Transfer the zucchini and bell peppers to separate plates and set aside.

Cover the bottom and sides of the prepared pan with a single layer of half of the eggplant slices, overlapping them. Spread half of the tomato paste on the first layer of eggplant and sprinkle with one-third of the thyme leaves, one-third of the garlic, and a grinding of black pepper. Add a layer of the bell peppers, using them all and covering as much of the bottom and sides as possible. Follow with a layer of zucchini, using it all. Sprinkle with another one-third each of the thyme and garlic. Add a layer of the rest of the eggplant, followed by the remaining tomato paste, thyme, and garlic and a generous grinding of pepper. Press down on the surface. Bake for 20 minutes.

Let cool to room temperature, about 1 hour. Place a serving plate, facedown, on top of the vegetable cake. Holding the plate tightly, carefully turn the pan upside down. Once it feels secure on the plate, remove the pan, foil, and parchment. Some of the juices will leak out but the cake should hold its shape. Garnish with a few sprigs of thyme, cut into wedges, and serve.

—— roasted brussels sprouts salad ——

SERVES 4

1 lb Brussels sprouts, trimmed and halved

1 cup diced bacon

1 to 2 Tbsp macadamia oil or coconut oil, melted

2 Tbsp extra-virgin olive oil

1 Tbsp balsamic vinegar

½ tsp hot mustard

Juice of ½ lime

½ tsp minced garlic

1 tsp sea salt

½ tsp freshly ground black pepper

10 cherry tomatoes, halved

Preheat the oven to 400°F. On a baking sheet, toss the Brussels sprouts and bacon in the macadamia oil to coat. Spread in a single layer and roast until tender and browned, about 30 minutes. Stir once, halfway through roasting.

In a small bowl, whisk together the olive oil, vinegar, mustard, lime juice, garlic, salt, and pepper.

In a medium bowl, combine the cherry tomatoes, warm Brussels sprouts, and dressing and toss to coat. Serve warm.

—— brussels sprouts with cranberries ——

SERVES 2

2 Tbsp macadamia oil or ghee

1 yellow onion, thinly sliced

20 brussels sprouts, shredded

2 garlic cloves, minced

1 tsp butter or ghee

½ tsp sea salt

¼ cup dried cranberries

1 tsp balsamic vinegar

Freshly ground black pepper

In a medium frying pan over medium heat, warm the macadamia oil. Add the onion and cook until soft and translucent, 7 to 8 minutes.

Add the Brussels sprouts to the pan, stir, and then add the garlic, butter, and salt. Cook for 2 to 3 minutes, stirring occasionally. Add the cranberries and vinegar and season with pepper. Stir and cook for 2 to 3 minutes longer. Serve warm.

cauliflower couscous

I make cauliflower couscous whenever I serve a hearty meat or fish tagine or Moroccan spiced lamb cutlets. It's fast and easy to prepare—but be sure not to overcook the cauliflower, or it will lose its crunch. You can use a variety of spice mixes for seasoning.

SERVES 3 OR 4

1 head cauliflower, cored and broken into florets

½ cup raw pistachios, plus more for garnish

2 Tbsp ghee

1 yellow onion, minced

2 garlic cloves, minced

Zest of 1 lemon, plus juice of ½ lemon

1 tsp sea salt

½ tsp freshly ground black pepper

½ tsp turmeric powder

½ tsp curry powder

3 Tbsp extra-virgin olive oil

Handful of chopped parsley

¼ cup pomegranate seeds

In a food processor, process the cauliflower into small crumbs. Transfer to a bowl and set aside. Then, grind the ½ cup pistachios into small crumbs (be careful not to overprocess, or you will make nut butter). Set aside.

In a large frying pan over medium heat, melt 1 Tbsp of the ghee. Add the onion and cook until soft, 7 to 8 minutes. Add the ground nuts, garlic, lemon zest, and remaining 1 Tbsp ghee to the pan and stir for 2 minutes. Add the salt, pepper, turmeric, and curry powder and cook, stirring for 1 minute longer. Add the cauliflower, stir to combine, and cook just until tender, 1 to 2 minutes. Drizzle with the lemon juice and olive oil and sprinkle with the parsley and pomegranate seeds. Serve warm, garnished with pistachios.

The pomegranate seeds can be replaced with diced dried fruit such as apricots, figs, or cranberries. Other nuts can be used instead of pistachios.

dukkah-spiced roasted pumpkin

Pumpkin and dukkah go really well together; this is a quick and easy way to pair them. Alternatively, toss the pumpkin in melted coconut oil and coat in dukkah before roasting in the oven. Sun-dried tomatoes add acidity and pumpkin seeds add a little crunch to the dish. Make extra to pack for lunch the next day.

SERVES 3

½ **small pumpkin, peeled and seeded**

1 **Tbsp coconut oil, melted**

2 **Tbsp dukkah**

½ **tsp sea salt**

¼ **cup sun-dried tomatoes, cut into slices**

1 **Tbsp pumpkin seeds**

Preheat the oven to 400°F.

Cut the pumpkin into ½-inch slices. Pile on a baking sheet and toss with the melted coconut oil. Spread the slices in a single layer and bake for 25 to 30 minutes. Sprinkle with the dukkah, salt, sun-dried tomatoes, and pumpkin seeds. Serve warm.

You can buy dukkah spice mix in most supermarkets and delis or make your own. Instead of throwing away the pumpkin skins, roast them for 40 to 45 minutes, or until crunchy, and season with some sea salt—better than potato chips!

nectarine & quail egg salad

Just by adding quail eggs and some fresh, sweet nectarines, you can transform a simple garden salad into a fancy dish. Free-range chicken eggs can easily be substituted.

SERVES 2

10 quail eggs, at room temperature

5 Tbsp extra-virgin olive oil

2 Tbsp white wine vinegar

10 basil leaves

½ tsp Dijon mustard

Sea salt and freshly ground black pepper

2 cups arugula

½ red bell pepper, seeded and thinly sliced

10 cherry tomatoes, halved

½ red onion, thinly sliced

2 nectarines, pitted and sliced

1 tsp black sesame seeds

Bring a medium saucepan of water to a boil. Gently immerse the quail eggs and cook for 5 minutes. Drain, rinse under cold water, peel, and cut in half. Set aside.

In a food processor or a blender, combine the olive oil, vinegar, basil, and mustard; season with salt and pepper; and process until smooth.

On a large serving platter, toss the arugula with the bell pepper, cherry tomatoes, and onion. Top with the quail eggs and nectarine slices and drizzle with the basil dressing. Sprinkle with a little more salt and the sesame seeds and serve.

You can also use white sesame seeds. Peaches can be used instead of nectarines.

grapefruit & fennel salad

When people come over for dinner, I make this salad because it looks so pretty and fresh on the table. Crispy, tangy, and bursting with flavor, it will brighten up any winter dinner and cool you off on a hot summer day. Pro tip: It goes really well with lamb cutlets.

SERVES 2

1 pink grapefruit

**2 Tbsp lemon juice, plus
1 tsp lemon zest**

2 Tbsp extra-virgin olive oil

1 tsp mayonnaise

½ tsp raw honey or maple syrup

Sea salt and freshly ground black pepper

½ fennel bulb, cored and thinly sliced or shaved

1 avocado, pitted, peeled, and sliced

¼ red onion, thinly sliced

3 cups mixed salad greens

Mint leaves and fennel fronds for garnish

Using a grater, zest the grapefruit and set the zest aside. Cut a thin slice off the base of the grapefruit so it sits flat on your cutting board. Slice down along the sides of the fruit, following the contours, to remove the white pith. Holding the grapefruit over a bowl to catch any juice, cut it into segments. Set the grapefruit segments aside.

Add 1 tsp of the reserved grapefruit zest, the lemon juice, lemon zest, olive oil, mayonnaise, and honey to the bowl with the grapefruit juice and whisk to combine. Season with salt and pepper.

On a large serving platter, arrange the grapefruit segments, fennel, avocado, onion, and greens. Drizzle with the dressing. Top with a few mint leaves and fennel fronds and serve immediately.

sage & pancetta sweet potato

Brown butter sauce is a favorite of mine, but you can use ghee if you're avoiding dairy as it's 95 percent fat with practically no milk solids. Olive oil can also be used, but you'll miss out on the gorgeous nutty flavor of brown butter.

SERVES 2

1 sweet potato, scrubbed and halved lengthwise

2 Tbsp extra-virgin olive oil

4 to 6 slices pancetta

2 Tbsp butter or ghee

2 garlic cloves, sliced

20 sage leaves

½ tsp sea salt

½ tsp freshly ground black pepper

Pinch of freshly grated nutmeg

Preheat the oven to 400°F. Line a baking sheet with parchment paper.

Place the sweet potato halves on the prepared baking sheet, cut-side up, and bake until very soft and the skin is browned, 35 to 40 minutes.

Meanwhile, in a medium frying pan over medium heat, warm 1 Tbsp of the olive oil. Add the pancetta and cook until crispy, about 2 minutes per side. Transfer the pancetta to paper towels to drain and reserve the fat in the pan.

About 5 minutes before the sweet potatoes are ready, place the frying pan back over medium heat. Add the remaining 1 Tbsp olive oil and the butter to the reserved fat. When the butter is melted, add the garlic, sage, salt, pepper, and nutmeg and cook until the butter foams, the garlic browns slightly, and the sage leaves turn crispy, 3 to 5 minutes.

Place a sweet potato half on each plate, drizzle with the butter sauce, making sure the sage leaves and garlic are evenly distributed. Serve with the crispy pancetta on the side.

moroccan eggplant salad

Eggplant is one my favorite vegetables to cook. I love its smoky, almost meaty flavor and silky, soft texture. It's particularly tasty with Middle Eastern spices, garlic, and lemon, which form the basis of this salad.

SERVES 4 TO 6

2 large eggplants

Sea salt

2 Tbsp coconut oil

2 tsp ghee

1 Tbsp extra-virgin olive oil, plus more for drizzling

1 red bell pepper, seeded and sliced

2 garlic cloves, chopped

1 tsp ground cumin

½ tsp ground coriander

½ tsp chili powder or red pepper flakes

Zest and juice of 1 lemon

4 plum tomatoes, quartered, seeded, and diced

1 red onion, thinly sliced

Chopped parsley for garnish

Slice the eggplants into ½-inch rounds. Arrange on a work surface and sprinkle liberally with 2 tsp salt. Let rest for 10 minutes to draw out some of the juices. (This will prevent them from soaking up too much oil during cooking.) Rinse with cold water and blot dry with paper towels.

In a large frying pan over medium-high heat, melt the coconut oil with the ghee until sizzling hot. Fry the eggplant in batches until dark golden brown but not black, 2 to 3 minutes per side. Transfer to a bowl and set aside.

Turn the heat to medium-low and add the 1 Tbsp olive oil to the same pan. Add the bell pepper and cook for about 3 minutes. Stir in the garlic, cumin, coriander, chili powder, and lemon zest and cook for 2 minutes, then transfer to the bowl with the eggplant. Add the tomatoes, onion, and lemon juice to the bowl; drizzle with a little olive oil; and toss to mix. Sprinkle with the parsley, season with salt, and serve warm or at room temperature.

> Make sure the eggplant is charred, as that's what gives this dish real depth and a smoky flavor that goes really well with grilled chicken or lamb.

& MEAT

roasted rib-eye with arugula chimichurri

This recipe is designed for two, so be prepared to share this chunky, juicy rib-eye. Along with the definitive parsley, chimichurri can be made with spinach or other dark green salad leaves instead of arugula. Store leftover chimichurri in an airtight container; it will keep for up to 3 days in the refrigerator.

SERVES 2

1¼ lb bone-in rib-eye steak

Olive oil for brushing

½ tsp sea salt

½ tsp freshly ground black pepper

1 tsp ghee

For the chimichurri

½ cup extra-virgin olive oil

½ cup chopped arugula

½ cup chopped parsley

2 Tbsp white wine vinegar

2 garlic cloves, diced

½ long red chile, seeded and diced

1 tsp lemon zest

½ tsp sea salt

Brush the steak with olive oil and sprinkle both sides with the salt and pepper. Let rest for 20 minutes to bring to room temperature.

Preheat the oven to 350°F. Place a grill pan over high heat.

Add the ghee to the grill pan and melt; once sizzling, add the steak. Sear until dark brown, 3 to 4 minutes per side. Transfer to a rimmed baking sheet and roast for 15 minutes for medium-rare. Transfer the steak to a cutting board, cover with aluminum foil, and let rest for 7 to 8 minutes.

Meanwhile, make the chimichurri: Combine the olive oil, arugula, parsley, vinegar, garlic, chile, lemon zest, and salt in a food processor and process to a thick paste.

Slice the steak and serve topped with the chimichurri.

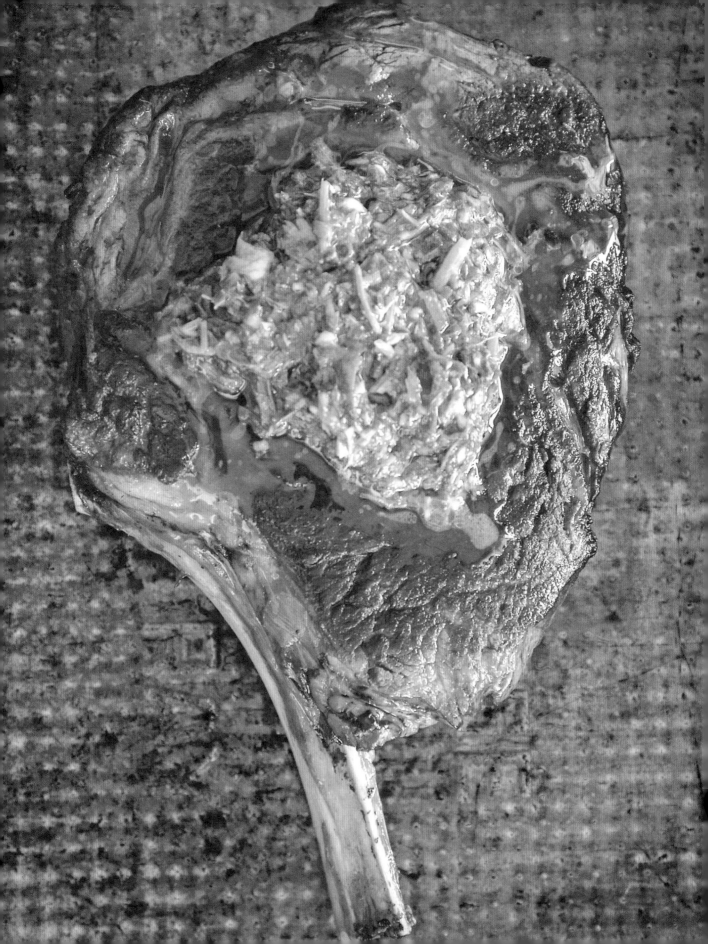

chicken, leek purée & macadamia crumbs

This is one of my favorite dishes to make for guests. They're always pleasantly startled by the contrast of flavors and textures: the velvety, almost sweet leek purée; the subtly salty chicken; and the zesty, crunchy macadamia crumbs. Be a Michelin-starred chef in your own kitchen.

SERVES 3

1 Tbsp extra-virgin olive oil

1 Tbsp Dijon mustard

1 tsp garlic powder

½ tsp sea salt

2 chicken breasts

For the leek purée

3 Tbsp ghee

2 leeks, pale and light green parts only, sliced and well rinsed

1 potato, peeled and cubed

¾ cup vegetable stock

¼ cup white wine

1 tsp sea salt

For the macadamia crumbs

½ cup macadamia nuts

1 garlic clove

Zest of 1 lemon, plus 2 Tbsp lemon juice

2 Tbsp macadamia or olive oil

½ tsp sea salt

1 tsp coconut oil

1 Tbsp oregano leaves

In a medium bowl, combine the olive oil, mustard, garlic powder, and salt and stir to mix well. Add the chicken and turn to coat. Set aside to marinate for 20 minutes.

To make the purée: In a medium saucepan over medium-high heat, melt the ghee. Add the leek, stirring occasionally, and cook for 10 minutes. Add the potato, vegetable stock, wine, and salt and bring to a boil. Turn the heat to medium and cook, uncovered, until the potato is soft, about 15 minutes. Let cool slightly, then transfer the contents of the pan to a food processor or blender and process until smooth. Return the mixture to the saucepan and set aside.

To make the crumbs: In a food processor, combine the macadamia nuts, garlic, and lemon zest and process to small crumbs. In a medium frying pan over medium heat, warm the macadamia oil. Add the macadamia mixture and salt. Cook, stirring every 15 seconds, until the nuts and garlic start to brown slightly, 3 to 4 minutes. Remove from the heat, add the lemon juice, and stir. Set aside.

In a large frying pan over medium heat, melt the coconut oil until sizzling hot. Add the chicken and cook until opaque throughout, about 5 minutes per side. Transfer to a plate and let rest for 2 to 3 minutes.

Gently rewarm the leek purée. Spread a spoonful of the purée on each plate. Slice the chicken and arrange on top of the purée, sprinkle each portion with 2 to 3 tsp of the macadamia crumbs and garnish with the oregano leaves. Serve immediately.

chicken & wild mushroom stew

In this mushroom-infused stew, the chicken is cooked until very tender. It's a perfect hearty dish to bring to the family dinner table.

SERVES 4

1 oz dried wild mushrooms

1 Tbsp ghee or coconut oil

1 yellow onion, sliced

½ cup diced bacon

1 celery rib, diced

½ lb chicken breast, diced

½ cup white wine

3 garlic cloves, chopped

2 cups chicken stock

3 bay leaves

Pinch of freshly ground nutmeg

½ tsp sea salt

½ tsp freshly ground black pepper

2 carrots, sliced

8 button mushrooms, brushed clean and sliced

1 zucchini, sliced

1 Tbsp arrowroot powder, dissolved in 2 Tbsp water

1 tsp lemon zest

2 Tbsp parsley leaves

In a small bowl, soak the dried mushrooms in 1 cup of boiling water for 10 minutes. Drain, reserving the soaking water. Set aside.

In a large saucepan over medium heat, melt the ghee. Add the onion and sauté for 5 minutes. Add the bacon and celery and cook for about 3 minutes. Add the chicken and cook, stirring, until the meat is slightly browned, about 5 minutes.

Add the soaked mushrooms and wine and raise the heat to let the liquid bubble away for a minute. Add the garlic, chicken stock, ½ cup of the reserved mushroom liquid, the bay leaves, nutmeg, salt, and pepper. Lower the heat to maintain a gentle simmer, cover, and cook for 40 minutes.

After 40 minutes, stir in the carrots and button mushrooms. Re-cover and simmer for 1 hour longer, stirring occasionally, then add the zucchini and arrowroot slurry. Stir and cook, uncovered, until thickened, about 10 minutes longer. Sprinkle with the lemon zest and parsley before serving.

Serve with steamed cauliflower, broccoli, or green beans. For a slightly higher-carbohydrate meal, serve with a side of sweet potato or pumpkin. Tapioca flour can be used instead of arrowroot.

braised cabbage rolls

This dish is an adaptation of traditional Ukrainian cabbage rolls made with minced meat, rice, and vegetables. It was one of my favorite family meals growing up. It takes a little effort to prepare the rolls, but they keep well refrigerated for a few days and are totally worth the effort.

MAKES 12 ROLLS

1 large head cabbage

½ lb ground pork

½ lb ground beef

½ cup ground hazelnuts or almonds

1 yellow onion, minced

3 garlic cloves, minced

2 Tbsp pine nuts

2 Tbsp extra-virgin olive oil

1 Tbsp gluten-free Worcestershire sauce

1 egg, beaten

2 Tbsp chopped parsley

2 tsp sweet paprika

1 tsp Dijon mustard

1½ tsp sea salt

½ tsp freshly ground black pepper

½ tsp red pepper flakes

One 28-oz can diced tomatoes, drained

1 tsp tomato paste

2 cups vegetable stock

3 bay leaves

1 star anise

Bring a large pot of water to a boil. Carefully place the whole cabbage head in the boiling water and cook for 6 to 8 minutes. Using tongs, transfer to a colander and rinse under cold water, reserving the boiling water. Carefully peel 12 large cabbage leaves from the head, cutting them off at the core. Leaves that aren't completely cooked can be returned to the boiling water for 1 to 2 minutes longer to soften. Place the leaves on a baking sheet. (Save the remaining cabbage for another use.)

Preheat the oven to 350°F.

In a medium bowl, combine the pork, beef, hazelnuts, onion, garlic, pine nuts, olive oil, Worcestershire, egg, parsley, paprika, mustard, salt, black pepper, and red pepper flakes. Using your hands, mix until well incorporated.

Trim off the thick part of the vein from each cooked cabbage leaf for easier rolling. Place 2 to 3 Tbsp of the meat mixture in the middle of each, fold in the sides, and roll up tightly. Place seam-side down in a deep casserole dish. Set aside.

In a medium saucepan over medium-high heat, combine the tomatoes, tomato paste, vegetable stock, bay leaves, and star anise and bring to a boil, stirring. Pour over the cabbage rolls, making sure some of the liquid gets under the rolls. Cover with aluminum foil or an ovenproof lid and bake for 20 minutes. Uncover and bake 10 minutes longer. Serve warm, with a spoonful of the tomato sauce from the baking dish on top.

> The nuts and egg can be omitted from this recipe. The rolls are traditionally served with a dollop of sour cream.

peppered beef skewers

As an Australian, I often make these skewers with kangaroo, but beef, lamb, or bison is just as delicious. Serve with roasted sweet potatoes or a nice green salad.

SERVES 6

For the marinade

½ cup extra-virgin olive oil

¼ cup red wine

2 Tbsp balsamic vinegar

2 Tbsp gluten-free Worcestershire sauce

1 tsp sea salt

1 tsp sweet paprika

½ tsp smoked paprika

½ tsp garlic powder

½ tsp ground coriander

½ tsp freshly ground black pepper

1 lb skirt steak or beef chuck, cut into 1-inch cubes

2 zucchini, cut into ½-inch slices

1 red bell pepper, seeded and cut into 1-inch squares

1 yellow bell pepper, seeded and cut into 1-inch squares

1 red onion, cut into 1-inch squares

2 Tbsp extra-virgin olive oil

To make the marinade: In a large bowl, whisk together the olive oil, wine, vinegar, Worcestershire, salt, both paprikas, garlic powder, coriander, and black pepper.

Add the meat to the bowl with the marinade and stir to coat. Let marinate for 30 minutes to 1 hour.

Soak 8 to 10 long bamboo skewers in water for 10 minutes, then drain.

Add the zucchini, bell peppers, and onion to the bowl with the meat and stir. Thread the meat and vegetables onto the skewers, leaving about ½ inch on each end. (Reserve any leftover vegetables to grill once the skewers are done.)

Prepare a gas or charcoal grill or heat a large grill pan to high and brush the rack or pan with the olive oil. Grill the skewers until nicely browned and grill-marked, 3 to 4 minutes on each side, covering the grill for 1 to 2 minutes of each interval. Let rest for a few minutes before serving warm.

poached chicken & coconut salad

Reach for this recipe for an easy, no-fuss dinner, or as a snack or party finger-food. It's spicy, yummy, and almost too easy to eat.

SERVES 4

2 cups vegetable stock

2 cups coconut milk

1 stalk lemongrass, peeled and cut into thirds

4 lime leaves

Zest of 1 lime

1 small red chile, seeded and thinly sliced

2 Tbsp fish sauce

¼ tsp sea salt

4 chicken breasts, cut into strips

For the dressing

¼ cup coconut cream

2 limes, finely chopped, plus juice of 1 lime

2 Tbsp fish sauce

1 tsp raw honey

For the salad

2 cups mixed lettuces

½ cup cilantro leaves

½ cup mint leaves

½ cup Thai basil leaves

1 cucumber, thinly sliced

1 long red chile, seeded and thinly sliced

½ cup thinly sliced green onions

1 mango, peeled, pitted, and sliced

Preheat the oven to 300°F.

In a medium saucepan over medium-high heat, combine the vegetable stock, coconut milk, lemongrass, lime leaves, lime zest, chile, fish sauce, and salt. Bring to a boil.

Place the chicken in a deep baking dish and pour the warm coconut mixture over to cover. Bake for 15 minutes.

Transfer the chicken to a plate or bowl to cool. (Save the poaching liquid for another use, if you like.)

To make the dressing: In a small bowl, whisk together the coconut cream, chopped lime, lime juice, fish sauce, and honey. Set aside.

To make the salad: In a bowl, using your hands, toss together the lettuce, cilantro, mint, basil, cucumber, chile, green onions, and mango to combine.

Divide the salad among individual plates. Top each with the poached chicken and drizzle with the coconut dressing to serve.

Omit the chile if avoiding nightshades. You can use any combination of Thai-friendly herbs in this salad: Thai or regular basil, Vietnamese or regular mint, cilantro, or chives. Visit your local Asian grocer for supplies. The lime leaves can be replaced with fresh lime peel or lemongrass.

macadamia & herb-crusted pork chops

SERVES 4

4 pork loin chops

Sea salt and freshly ground black pepper

1 cup macadamia nuts

1 garlic clove, minced

½ cup chopped parsley

¼ cup extra-virgin olive oil

1 tsp ghee

Preheat the oven to 350°F. Season the pork chops with salt and pepper and let rest at room temperature for 30 to 45 minutes.

In a food processor, grind the macadamia nuts, garlic, parsley, olive oil, and a pinch of salt into a thick paste.

In a large frying pan over medium-high heat, melt the ghee until sizzling hot. Add the pork chops and sear for 1 minute on each side. Transfer to a plate and let cool. Press a thin layer of the macadamia paste on one side of each chop, and place on a baking sheet, paste-side up. Bake until the crust is golden brown and crispy, 12 to 15 minutes. Serve warm.

harissa-almond meatballs

SERVES 3 OR 4

⅔ cup blanched almonds

1¼ lb ground lamb

2 to 3 Tbsp harissa

⅔ cup dried currants or cranberries

1½ tsp sea salt

½ tsp freshly ground black pepper

1 Tbsp coconut oil

Preheat the oven to 350°F. In a medium frying pan over medium heat, toast the almonds, stirring frequently, until lightly browned, 4 to 5 minutes.

Transfer the almonds to a food processor and process (or use a mortar and pestle to crush them) into small crumbs. In a large mixing bowl, combine the crushed almonds with the lamb, harissa, currants, salt, and pepper. Using wet hands, roll the mixture into golf ball–size meatballs and set aside on a plate.

In large frying pan over medium-high heat, melt the coconut oil. Brown the meatballs on all sides, about 5 minutes total, working in batches. Transfer to a baking sheet and bake for 10 to 15 minutes. Their internal temperature should be 155° to 160°F when done. Serve warm.

A combination of ground pork and beef can be used instead of lamb. If using dried fruit larger than currants, chop them roughly.

chicken larb salad

SERVES 4

3 Tbsp coconut oil

1 stalk lemongrass, peeled and diced

1 long red chile, seeded and diced

2 Tbsp chopped cilantro stems

3 to 4 lime leaves (optional)

One 2-inch piece ginger, peeled and diced

1 lb ground chicken

2 garlic cloves, minced

1 tsp lime zest, plus juice of ½ lime

3 Tbsp fish sauce

1 Tbsp coconut aminos

Pinch of sea salt

¼ cup raw cashews

¼ cup coconut flakes

For the dressing

2 Tbsp extra-virgin olive oil

1 tsp grated palm sugar or honey

3 Tbsp lime juice

1½ Tbsp fish sauce

1 small red chile, seeded and finely diced

1 tsp sesame oil

¼ large head red cabbage, shredded

1 large carrot, grated

½ white onion, thinly sliced

2 Tbsp cilantro leaves

Handful of herbs

½ cup fried shallots (optional)

In a large frying pan or wok over medium-high heat, melt the coconut oil until sizzling hot. Add the lemongrass, chile, cilantro stems, lime leaves (if using), and ginger and stir-fry until fragrant, about 1 minute.

Add the chicken, garlic, and lime zest. Cook, stirring and breaking apart the meat with a wooden spatula, until the chicken is opaque throughout, 2 to 3 minutes. Add the fish sauce, coconut aminos, lime juice, and salt. Stir and cook until the flavors come together, about 5 minutes longer.

Meanwhile, in a small frying pan over medium heat, toast the cashews for 2 to 3 minutes. Use a mortar and pestle to grind into small crumbs. Add the coconut flakes to the same pan over medium heat and cook, stirring constantly, until toasted and golden brown, about 1 minute. Set aside.

To make the dressing: In a small bowl, whisk together the olive oil, palm sugar, lime juice, fish sauce, red chile, and sesame oil. Set aside.

In a salad bowl combine the cabbage, carrot, onion, cilantro leaves, and herbs and toss to mix. Add the cooked chicken and the dressing to the salad. Toss to combine and top with the toasted cashews and coconut flakes, and the fried shallots, if desired, before serving.

Fried shallots can be purchased from the Asian section of supermarkets. I try to use cilantro stems when frying chicken, as it's a nice way to use up that part of the herb. The best herbs for this salad are cilantro, mint, and Thai basil.

─── pulled-pork tacos feast ───

This was the last main dish I cooked while testing for the cookbook, so I invited a few friends over to enjoy my Mexican feast in celebration. We polished off every single bite and the menu got a massive tick of approval! The trick is to plan ahead, as the pork takes a few hours to cook and the cashews need to soak for up to 6 hours. I make the sides in the last hour of pork cooking time, but you could easily prepare this spread over two days.

SERVES 6 TO 8

For the pulled pork

1 Tbsp ghee

2¼ lb pork shoulder, cut into ¾-inch cubes

1 large yellow onion, thinly sliced

2 cups chicken stock

½ cup white wine

3 Tbsp tomato paste

1½ tsp smoked paprika

1½ tsp ground cumin

1 tsp ground coriander

3 bay leaves

1 star anise

1 tsp sea salt

1 tsp freshly ground black pepper

2 Tbsp balsamic vinegar

Zest and juice of 1 lime

1 Tbsp coconut sugar or raw honey

To make the pulled pork: In a large Dutch oven or casserole dish over medium-high heat, melt the ghee until sizzling hot. Add the pork and cook for about 5 minutes, stirring to sear on all sides. Add the onion, stir, and cook for 1 minute before adding the chicken stock, wine, tomato paste, paprika, cumin, coriander, bay leaves, star anise, salt, and pepper. Stir and bring to boil, then turn the heat to low and simmer, covered, stirring every 30 minutes, for 3 hours.

After 2 hours and 45 minutes, preheat the oven to 400°F. After 3 hours, use two forks to pull the meat into shreds in the Dutch oven. Add the vinegar, lime zest, and coconut sugar and stir to mix well. Transfer everything in the pot to a roasting tray and roast, uncovered, until the pork is browned and caramelized, 20 to 25 minutes. Drizzle with the lime juice and set aside, covered to keep warm.

Continued

1 cup cashews, soaked in water
for 6 hours

2 garlic cloves

3 shallots, diced

1 long red chile, seeded and diced

½ cup extra-virgin olive oil

1 Tbsp tomato paste

3 tsp ground coriander

1 tsp smoked paprika

1 tsp sea salt

1 cup water

Juice of ½ lime

For the guacamole

2 ripe avocados, pitted and peeled

1 Tbsp chopped cilantro

½ garlic clove, grated

Juice of ½ lime

½ tsp sea salt

½ tsp freshly ground black pepper

For the tomato salsa

4 medium tomatoes, seeded and
diced

½ red onion, minced

1 long red chile, seeded and minced

2 Tbsp red wine vinegar

2 Tbsp extra-virgin olive oil

20 small lettuce leaves,
washed and dried

To make the satay: Drain the cashews and place in a food processor with the garlic, shallots, and chile. Process into small crumbs and set aside.

In a medium saucepan over medium-high heat, warm the olive oil and then add the cashew mixture. Add the tomato paste, coriander, paprika, and salt. Cook for 3 to 4 minutes, stirring frequently. Gradually add the water while stirring the mixture. Turn the heat to low and cook until the sauce is thickened and caramelized, 6 to 8 minutes. Remove from the heat and stir in the lime juice. Set aside.

To make the guacamole: In a medium bowl, mash the avocados, cilantro, garlic, lime juice, salt, and pepper with a fork. Set aside.

To make the salsa: In a medium bowl, combine the tomatoes, onion, chile, vinegar, and olive oil. Set aside.

Pile some of the pulled pork in each lettuce leaf and top with the salsa, guacamole, and a small dollop of the satay. Serve immediately.

asian chicken cakes

Fragrant and full of zesty flavors, these chicken cakes are like savory candy. Make as part of an Asian-inspired dinner party or as a main dish with sautéed greens and cucumber salad. Dip in my Asian Twang dressing (page 196) before popping in your mouth.

MAKES 12 TO 14 CAKES

1¾ lb ground chicken

2 eggs

1 long red chile, seeded and minced

2 garlic cloves, minced

2 Tbsp chopped cilantro

1 Tbsp chopped Thai basil, plus a handful of small sprigs

3 Tbsp thinly sliced green onion

One 2-inch piece ginger, peeled and grated

2 Tbsp fish sauce

1 tsp sesame oil

Zest of 1 lime, plus 2 Tbsp lime juice

2 Tbsp coconut oil

2 cucumbers, sliced into ribbons

In a large mixing bowl, combine the chicken, eggs, chile, garlic, cilantro, chopped basil, green onion, ginger, fish sauce, sesame oil, lime zest, and lime juice. Using your hands, mix the ingredients thoroughly. Roll into golf ball–size rounds, place on a plate, and flatten slightly.

In a large frying pan over medium-high heat, melt the coconut oil until sizzling hot. Add the chicken cakes and cook until opaque throughout, 5 to 7 minutes per side. Serve warm, garnished with the cucumber and Thai basil sprigs.

You can use the same recipe for ground pork and beef instead of chicken. Store for up to 3 days refrigerated and for up to 1 month frozen. They can be added to curry sauces and broken into chunks for omelettes.

mustard-thyme quail

My favorite thing about quail is that you can have the whole bird to yourself and pull it apart, biting the succulent, tasty meat right off the bones. There's nothing like licking oozing juices off your fingers.

SERVES 6

For the marinade

½ cup extra-virgin olive oil

2 Tbsp lemon juice, plus zest of 1 lemon

2 Tbsp thyme leaves

2 garlic cloves, minced

1 tsp Dijon mustard

½ tsp turmeric powder

1½ tsp sea salt

½ tsp freshly ground black pepper

For the quail

6 quails

12 thyme sprigs

6 garlic cloves

6 slices lemon

Preheat the oven to 375°F.

To make the marinade: In a food processor, combine the olive oil, lemon juice, lemon zest, thyme, garlic, mustard, tumeric, salt, and pepper and process until well blended.

Rub the marinade all over the quail bodies and fill the cavities. Set aside at room temperature for 15 minutes.

Stuff 2 sprigs of thyme, a garlic clove, and a slice of lemon inside the body cavity of each quail. Tie the legs together with a piece of butcher's twine. Place the quail in a deep roasting pan and bake for 35 minutes. Transfer to a wire rack, tent with aluminum foil, and let rest for 5 to 10 minutes before serving.

> You can use the same marinade to roast chicken. Bake leeks and carrots on the lower oven shelf for a perfect side dish.

lemony harissa lamb chops

Serve these lamb chops (pictured opposite) with roasted pumpkin and an arugula salad. Ask your butcher to trim, or "French," the rack.

SERVES 2 OR 3

1 rack of lamb, Frenched

1 tsp sea salt

½ tsp freshly ground black pepper

½ tsp ground cumin

½ tsp sweet paprika

1 tsp coconut oil

2 Tbsp pine nuts

¼ cup Lemony Harissa (page 176)

2 Tbsp cilantro leaves

1 long red chile, seeded and thinly sliced

Preheat the oven to 350°F.

In a small bowl, stir together the salt, black pepper, cumin, and paprika and rub all over the lamb.

In a large frying pan over medium-high heat, melt the coconut oil. Add the lamb and sear until nicely browned, about 3 minutes per side.

Transfer the lamb to a roasting pan and roast for 12 minutes. Meanwhile, place the pine nuts on a baking sheet and toast for 2 minutes, stirring once. When the lamb is done, let it rest for 5 minutes before slicing between the bones into individual chops.

Arrange the chops on each plate, drizzle with the harissa, and sprinkle with the pine nuts, cilantro, and sliced chile. Serve immediately.

curried lamb chops

SERVES 4

½ cup coconut cream

2 garlic cloves, minced

1 Tbsp coconut aminos

1½ Tbsp curry powder

½ tsp ground coriander

½ tsp ground cumin

½ tsp red pepper flakes

½ tsp sea salt

12 lamb chops, Frenched

1 Tbsp coconut oil

In a small bowl, combine the coconut cream, garlic, coconut aminos, curry powder, coriander, cumin, red pepper flakes, and salt. Coat the lamb with the mixture and let marinate for 20 minutes.

In a large frying pan over medium-high heat, melt the coconut oil. Add the lamb and cook for 3 minutes on each side for medium to medium-rare. Let rest for a few minutes before serving.

my famous lasagna

This is the most popular recipe on my web site, so I simply had to include it in my cookbook. It's delicious! No other commentary needed.

SERVES 6

For the sauce

2 Tbsp extra-virgin olive oil

1 yellow onion, diced

Sea salt

1 tsp ghee

1 lb ground beef

⅔ cup dry red wine

3 garlic cloves, minced

½ tsp freshly ground black pepper

½ tsp sweet paprika

3 cups diced tomatoes

1 eggplant, cut into ½-inch slices

1 tsp sea salt

7 Tbsp extra-virgin olive oil

2 parsnips, peeled and thinly sliced

1 tsp ghee

½ cup torn basil leaves

6 button mushrooms, sliced

2 cups baby spinach

3 zucchini, sliced into thin ribbons

Freshly ground black pepper

1½ cups ricotta cheese (optional)

3 Tbsp grated Parmesan cheese (optional)

Cherry tomatoes, halved, for garnish

Preheat the oven to 350°F.

To make the sauce: In a large saucepan over medium heat, warm the olive oil. Add the onion with a pinch of salt and cook for 5 minutes. Add the ghee and beef and turn the heat to high. Use a wooden spoon to stir and break the meat into small pieces. Cook until browned, 5 to 6 minutes.

Add the wine, garlic, black pepper, paprika and 1 tsp salt and cook for 3 to 4 minutes. Add the tomatoes and bring to a boil, then turn the heat to low and simmer for 10 minutes.

Meanwhile, sprinkle the eggplant with the salt and set aside for 10 minutes to draw out the juices. Rinse and pat dry.

Brush the bottom of a deep casserole with 2 Tbsp of the olive oil. Layer the parsnips on the bottom of the dish, overlapping them. Bake for 10 minutes.

In a large frying pan over medium heat, warm 2 Tbsp olive oil with the ghee. Fry the eggplant in batches until browned, about 3 minutes per side. Add more olive oil as needed.

Remove the casserole from the oven and layer in the following order on top of the parsnips: one-third of the sauce, the eggplant slices, the basil (save a little for garnish), the mushrooms, the remaining two-thirds of the sauce, the spinach, the zucchini, the remaining olive oil, and a sprinkle of black pepper. Press down and bake until bubbling, 35 to 40 minutes. If using the ricotta and Parmesan, add on top of the lasagna after 20 minutes of baking. Turn the oven temperature to 400°F for the final 10 to 15 minutes. Let cool slightly, then cut into big squares and garnish each with a sprinkle of basil and a few cherry tomatoes. Serve warm.

filet mignon, leeks & mushrooms

Filet mignon is one of the most tender cuts of beef, and requires little effort in the kitchen. Many believe that it's sacrilege to cook it beyond medium or medium-rare, and that it needs no marinating. All it needs is a couple of beautiful complementary sides.

SERVES 4

Two 4- to 5-oz filet mignon steaks

Sea salt and freshly ground black pepper

For the leeks

2 Tbsp coconut oil

2 leeks, sliced and well rinsed

1 tsp whole-grain mustard

Pinch of sea salt

For the mushrooms

1 cup dried porcini mushrooms

2 Tbsp extra-virgin olive oil

1½ tsp ghee

3 cups brushed clean and sliced button mushrooms

3 garlic cloves, minced

1 tsp lemon zest, plus 1 Tbsp lemon juice

½ tsp sea salt

½ cup white wine

1 tsp tapioca flour dissolved in 1 Tbsp warm water

1 tsp coconut oil

Take the steaks out of the refrigerator, season with a little salt and pepper and set aside for about 30 minutes to come to room temperature.

To make the leeks: In a medium saucepan over medium heat, melt the coconut oil. Add the leeks, mustard, and salt and cook for 12 to 15 minutes, stirring occasionally.

Meanwhile, make the mushrooms: In a small bowl, soak the dried mushrooms in 1 cup of boiling water for 10 minutes. Drain, reserving the soaking water.

In a large frying pan over medium heat, warm the olive oil and 1 tsp of the ghee. Add the soaked porcinis and button mushrooms, garlic, lemon zest, and salt and cook until the mushrooms are slightly browned, 3 to 4 minutes. Add the wine and ½ cup of the reserved mushroom-soaking water. Turn the heat to high to bring to a boil. Turn the heat to medium and simmer for 3 minutes before adding the tapioca slurry, lemon juice, and remaining ½ tsp ghee. Stir until the sauce thickens. Remove from the heat. Transfer to a bowl and set aside.

In another medium frying pan over high heat, melt the coconut oil until sizzling hot. Cook the steaks for 3 to 4 minutes per side for medium-rare to medium. Let rest for 2 minutes. Top each steak with a large spoonful of the leeks and sautéed mushrooms. Serve hot.

mackerel plaki

Take a trip to a Greek island with this traditional baked fish recipe. The Greeks often make it with mackerel, but any other medium-size whole fish can be used. Mackerel has a pretty strong taste, but here it's beautifully mellowed by sweet tomatoes and peppers, garlic, onions, and wine. This recipe uses larger mackerel fish, but you can easily make this with six to eight smaller fish. Have your fishmonger clean and gut them for you. Serve with a large green salad or grilled zucchini, asparagus, or sweet potatoes.

SERVES 2

¼ cup extra-virgin olive oil

2 small yellow onions, sliced

1 large red bell pepper, seeded and sliced

Sea salt

2 whole mackerel, cleaned and gutted

3 garlic cloves, minced

2 Tbsp chopped parsley

1 pint cherry tomatoes, halved

3 bay leaves

2 medium carrots, thinly sliced

Zest and juice of 1 lemon

½ tsp freshly ground black pepper

1 cup dry white wine

Preheat the oven to 350°F. Line a rimmed baking sheet with two pieces of aluminum foil, leaving an overhang of about 1 inch on each end.

In a large frying pan over medium heat, warm the olive oil. Add the onions, bell pepper, and a pinch of salt and cook until softened and slightly caramelized, about 15 minutes.

Stuff the fish with a big pinch each of the garlic and parsley. Place half of the cooked onions and bell pepper on the bottom of the prepared baking sheet and top with half of the cherry tomatoes, a little more garlic, the bay leaves, and half each of the carrots, lemon zest, and lemon juice. Sprinkle with the pepper and 1 tsp salt.

Place the fish on top of the vegetables and cover with the remaining onions and peppers, cherry tomatoes, garlic, parsley, carrots, and lemon zest. Drizzle with the remaining lemon juice and pour over the wine. Cover with another piece of foil and bake for 20 minutes, letting the fish steam inside. Remove the top layer of foil and bake for 20 minutes longer, uncovered, until the vegetables are caramelized and nicely browned. Serve immediately.

basque sardines

This dish was inspired by the grilled sardines I had in Biarritz, a beautiful coastal town in the Basque region of France. The original dish didn't have the same seasoning as this one and the sardines were grilled whole, but I feel it still captures that gorgeous warm evening at the fisherman's wharf with my best friend, combining the taste of the sea with Basque flavors of paprika, garlic, olive oil, and herbs. This dish pairs nicely with a glass of good rosé.

SERVES 2

10 sardines, cleaned and gutted

3 Tbsp olive oil or macadamia oil

2 garlic cloves, minced

2 Tbsp chopped parsley

1 tsp sweet paprika

½ tsp sea salt

Pinch of freshly ground black pepper

1 Tbsp ghee

Lemon wedges for squeezing

Flatten the sardines and remove the backbones by opening the gut cavity and laying the fish on a cutting board, skin-side up. Press down on the backbone with the palm of your hand from the head to the tail. Turn the fish over and peel off the backbone. You can use a pair of scissors to cut it out if it's stubborn. Don't worry if you miss a few small bones. (You can also ask your fishmonger to do this step.)

In a small frying pan over low heat, warm the olive oil. Add the garlic and cook until golden brown, 4 to 5 minutes. Stir to avoid burning. Transfer the garlic to a paper towel to drain, then mix in a small bowl with the parsley, paprika, salt, and pepper. Set aside.

In a grill pan over medium-high heat, melt the ghee until sizzling hot. Place the flattened sardines in the pan, skin-side down, and cook for 2 to 3 minutes. Using a metal spatula, carefully flip and cook on the second side for 30 seconds longer, just to slightly brown the flesh.

Serve sprinkled with the garlic-parsley mixture and a few squeezes of lemon juice.

oysters five ways

Succulent, juicy, salty, and full of iron, zinc, copper, vitamin D, and good omega-3 fatty acids, oysters are on the top of both nutritional and food connoisseurs' must-have lists. Next time you get a platter to go with a crisp glass of white wine, try one of these dressings inspired by my favorite world cuisines. Simply dice and mix all of the ingredients in a small dipping bowl and serve with oysters on the half shell.

ENOUGH FOR A DOZEN OYSTERS

MEXICAN

2 Tbsp extra-virgin olive oil

1½ Tbsp lime juice

4 slices pickled jalapeño, chopped

1 Tbsp chopped cilantro

¼ tsp ground cumin

FRENCH

1½ Tbsp extra-virgin olive oil

1 Tbsp red wine vinegar

1 shallot, minced

¼ tsp ground coriander

Pinch of sea salt

ASIAN

1½ Tbsp extra-virgin olive oil

1 Tbsp lime juice

1 tsp peeled and grated ginger

1 tsp thinly sliced or seeded and minced red chile

1 tsp sesame oil

1 tsp fish sauce

½ tsp grated palm sugar or raw honey

ITALIAN

2 Tbsp extra-virgin olive oil

1 Tbsp balsamic or white wine vinegar

½ tomato, seeded and diced

2 green or Kalamata olives, pitted and minced

½ Tbsp chopped parsley or basil

Pinch of sea salt

RUSSIAN

1½ Tbsp extra-virgin olive oil

1 Tbsp lemon juice

1 Tbsp diced cucumber

1 tsp chopped dill

Pinch of sea salt and freshly ground pepper

Fish roe for garnish

MEXICAN

ASIAN

RUSSKI

FRENCH

Italian

lemongrass & white wine mussels

This dish is special to me, as it's one of the first meals my partner ever cooked for me and it earned him quite a few brownie points. He still cooks it for me to this day, and I love it so much I asked if I could adapt and use the recipe in the cookbook. It's so fresh and full of flavor; plus, mussels are very nutritious. Normally, mussels are served with a fresh baguette or some thick-cut fries to soak up the liquid, but you can also serve a side of steamed broccoli or snow peas to add to the broth once all the mussels are gone.

SERVES 2

1 Tbsp coconut oil

3 green onions, diced

½ red chile, seeded and sliced

1 stalk lemongrass, pale part only, peeled and diced

2 garlic cloves, chopped

1½ cups dry white wine

1½ Tbsp fish sauce

1 cup vegetable stock

¼ lb mussels, scrubbed and debearded

Handful of mint leaves

Handful of Thai or regular basil leaves

1 lemon, halved

In a large soup pot or a wide saucepan with a lid over medium-low heat, melt the coconut oil. Add the green onions, chile, lemongrass, and garlic and sauté until everything softens, about 2 minutes.

Turn the heat to medium-high and add the wine and fish sauce. Simmer to reduce the liquid for about 30 seconds, then add the vegetable stock. Bring back to a boil and add the mussels. Stir to cover all the mussels with the broth, turn the heat to medium, cover the pan, and cook for 5 to 6 minutes. Stir again halfway through cooking to rotate the bottom and top layers of mussels. Remove from the heat when most of the mussels have opened. Discard any that fail to open.

Stir in the mint and basil, making sure they get all the way to the bottom. Squeeze over 1 to 2 Tbsp lemon juice. Serve in the pot with tongs and a spoon for the broth, or in individual bowls.

> When buying mussels, look for closed shells. If open, tap or squeeze them; if they close or move, it indicates that the mussel is alive. Avoid or discard any that do not respond. Also avoid any mussels that smell "fishy" or have broken shells. The color of the flesh indicates whether the mussel is female (orange meat) or male (white meat).

macadamia-crusted fish fingers

This is my modern take on an all-time favorite. The fish is partially covered with a mixture of healthful macadamia nuts, parsley, and garlic, making it delicate and fragrant. Tartar sauce is replaced with creamy red cabbage coleslaw, spiked with the faint anise aroma of tarragon, which complements the fish beautifully. It's a little bit spring and a little bit French, really.

SERVES 2

For the coleslaw

¼ **head red cabbage, thinly sliced**

1 medium carrot, grated

½ **medium red onion, thinly sliced**

1 Tbsp extra-virgin olive oil

1 Tbsp white wine vinegar

1 Tbsp mayonnaise

Small handful of tarragon leaves

Sea salt and freshly ground pepper

For the fish fingers

Coconut oil for greasing

1 lb white fish fillets, such as ling cod or haddock

1 tsp sea salt

1 cup macadamia nuts

2 Tbsp extra-virgin olive oil

2 garlic cloves, chopped

Zest of 1 lemon, plus lemon wedges for serving

2 Tbsp chopped parsley

Pinch of freshly ground black pepper

To make the coleslaw: In a medium bowl, combine the cabbage, carrot, onion, olive oil, vinegar, mayonnaise, and tarragon and stir to mix well. Season with salt and pepper and refrigerate until ready to serve.

To make the fish fingers: Preheat the oven to 400°F. Grease a baking sheet with coconut oil and line with a piece of parchment paper.

Slice the fish fillets into ½-inch strips. Sprinkle with the salt and set aside.

In a food processor or blender, combine the macadamias, olive oil, garlic, lemon zest, parsley, and pepper and process into fine crumbs. Using your fingers, press the crumb mixture onto the fish, coating the top of each slice in a generous layer.

Place the fillets on the prepared baking sheet, leaving some space in between. Bake until the crumbed mixture turns golden brown and crisp and the fish is opaque throughout, about 12 minutes.

Serve the fish fingers with the coleslaw and lemon wedges alonside.

You can bake whole breaded fish fillets instead of smaller strips. Tarragon can be omitted or replaced with fresh dill, which also goes well with fish and seafood. Those avoiding eggs can leave out the mayonnaise and add extra lemon juice and olive oil for the coleslaw dressing.

lime & cilantro butter scallops

Serve this dish (pictured opposite) to dinner guests or as a special starter at a family Sunday lunch and take everyone on a mini trip to the Caribbean. You can't go wrong with the combination of sweet, plump scallops and fresh citrus butter.

MAKES 12 SHELLS

12 scallops on the half shell

2 Tbsp Lime & Cilantro Butter (page 194)

½ lime

Sea salt and freshly ground black pepper

Preheat the oven to 400°F.

Arrange the scallops in their shells on a baking sheet and top each with ½ tsp of the butter. Bake for 4 to 5 minutes. Squeeze some lime juice on top, sprinkle with salt and pepper, and serve hot.

> Those who don't like cilantro (some people have a gene that makes it taste like soap) can use parsley instead. If avoiding all dairy, use olive oil instead of butter and make a salsa-like dressing instead.

lime & sesame tuna tartare

Serve with sliced radishes, lettuce leaves, and/or my Tahini Crackers on page 172.

SERVES 2

1 Tbsp coconut aminos

1 Tbsp fish sauce

2 Tbsp lime juice, plus 1 tsp, and 1 tsp lime zest

1 tsp sesame oil

1 tsp extra-virgin olive oil

½ lb sashimi-grade tuna

1 Tbsp minced chives

1 Tbsp toasted sesame seeds

1 avocado, pitted and peeled

1 Tbsp chopped cilantro

Generous pinch of sea salt

In a medium bowl, whisk together the coconut aminos, fish sauce, 2 Tbsp lime juice, lime zest, sesame oil, and olive oil. Set aside.

Cut the tuna into small cubes. Add to the bowl with the dressing, along with the chives and sesame seeds. Stir to coat and set aside.

In a small bowl, combine the avocado with the 1 tsp lime juice, cilantro, and salt. Mash with a fork. Divide the tuna mixture between small plates or bowls, top with the mashed avocado, and serve immediately.

red curry prawns

Leave your manners at the door and get a bowl of water ready, because you'll be licking your fingers like it's going out of style with this dish. This is my favorite way to prepare fresh prawns, and my friends absolutely love it. I like to marinate and cook the prawns in their shells because it gives them a rich flavor when grilled and protects the flesh from overcooking. The recipe makes more curry paste than you need.

SERVES 4

For the red curry paste

2 shallots, chopped

3 garlic cloves, chopped

2 long red chiles, seeded and chopped

1 stalk lemongrass, peeled and sliced

One 1-inch piece galangal, peeled and grated

One 1-inch turmeric root, peeled and grated

6 lime leaves

2 Tbsp chopped cilantro stems

2 Tbsp extra-virgin olive oil

1 Tbsp fish sauce

½ tsp palm or coconut sugar

1½ lb large prawns

½ cup coconut cream

Juice of ½ lime

Pinch of sea salt

Olive oil for brushing

Lime wedges, fresh cilantro sprigs, and red chile slices for serving

To make the curry paste: In a food processor, combine the shallots, garlic, chiles, lemongrass, galangal, turmeric, lime leaves, cilantro, olive oil, fish sauce, and sugar. Process into as smooth a paste as possible, about 3 minutes. (Store, refrigerated and covered with a layer of olive oil, for up to 7 days.)

Grip the body of a prawn in one hand and twist the head off with the other. Repeat with all the prawns. (Discard the heads or save them to make stock.) Make a deep cut along each belly almost all the way through to the shell but not quite. Open it like a book and press down so it's flat. Remove the dark vein running down the length of each prawn and rinse.

In a bowl, toss the butterflied prawns with 2 Tbsp of the curry paste, the coconut cream, lime juice, and salt until well coated. Let marinate in the refrigerator for 4 to 5 hours.

Preheat a grill pan until very hot and brush with olive oil. Place the prawns flesh-side down and cook for 3 minutes. Flip; the flesh should be opaque throughout. Cook on the shell side for 1 minute longer. Serve immediately with lime wedges, cilantro, and sliced chiles.

rosemary salt-baked fish

This traditional Spanish method of baking fish in salt keeps the flesh perfectly cooked and moist. Though it seems like the dish will turn out extremely salty, the fish absorbs only a subtle flavor of salt and rosemary, leaving the taste of the flesh intact. It looks impressive, almost theatrical, when you carve away chunks of the salt blanket, but the actual cooking method is ridiculously simple. Serve with a salad, such as arugula, fennel, orange, and olive.

SERVES 4

Olive oil for greasing

2 lb table salt

2 Tbsp chopped rosemary, plus 6 to 8 sprigs

¼ cup water

1 egg

One 3-lb whole red snapper

Lemon wedges for serving

Preheat the oven to 400°F. Grease a baking sheet with olive oil and line with a sheet of parchment paper.

In a large bowl, mix together the salt, chopped rosemary, water, and egg. Set aside.

Wash the snapper and pat it dry. Place several sprigs of rosemary in the body cavity. Place half of the salt mixture in the middle of the prepared baking sheet. Center the fish on top and cover with the remaining salt mixture. The salt mixture should be slightly moist, so you can mold it around the fish.

Bake until the salt crust has turned golden brown and hard, 20 to 25 minutes.

Transfer the fish to a serving platter, garnish with a few more rosemary sprigs, and serve with the lemon wedges on the side. Carve the fish at the table; the salt crust will break away in large pieces. Peel the scales away and enjoy the moist, flavorful fish.

When buying snapper, ask your fishmonger to remove the guts and clean the fish but to leave the scales on. This is a protective layer from the salt. Once cooked, the fish will stay warm inside the salt blanket for a little while.

mexican tuna steaks

SERVES 2

Two tuna steaks, each about 5 oz and ½ inch thick

Sea salt and freshly ground black pepper

Olive oil for drizzling

For the sweet and spicy peppers

3 Tbsp extra-virgin olive oil

1 medium red onion, sliced

1 red bell pepper, seeded and thinly sliced

1 large garlic clove, minced

1 Tbsp apple cider vinegar

½ tsp sweet paprika

½ tsp ground cumin

Pinch of sea salt

Pinch of red pepper flakes

2 Tbsp water

For the avocado salsa

1 large avocado, pitted, peeled, and chopped

2 Tbsp chopped cilantro

Juice of ½ lime

Pinch of sea salt

2 Tbsp macadamia oil or coconut oil

1 tsp butter

1 tsp ground coriander

Zest and juice of 1 lime

Rinse the tuna and pat dry. Place on a plate, sprinkle on both sides with a little salt and pepper, and drizzle with olive oil. Set aside to bring to room temperature.

To make the peppers: In a medium frying pan over medium heat, warm the olive oil. Add the onion and bell pepper, cover, and cook for 5 minutes, stirring a few times. Add the garlic, vinegar, paprika, cumin, salt, red pepper flakes, and water. Stir and cook until the onion and bell pepper are softened and slightly browned, about 5 minutes longer. Transfer to a plate and wipe the frying pan clean.

While the peppers are cooking, make the salsa: In a bowl, combine the avocado and cilantro. Season with the lime juice and salt. Set aside.

In the medium frying pan over high heat, warm the macadamia oil with the butter until sizzling hot. Add the coriander and lime zest and stir.

Add the tuna steaks to the pan. Turn the heat to medium and cook for 2 minutes. Flip, turn the heat to high to sear the other side, then turn the heat to medium again and cook for 2 minutes. Drizzle with the lime juice. Cook to your desired doneness. Spoon the sauce over the steaks while they're cooking.

Place a tuna steak on each plate. Spoon some of the avocado salsa and the peppers on top of each. Drizzle with a little extra-virgin olive oil. Serve immediately.

> Look for pole-caught albacore or skipjack tuna, and avoid the more vulnerable bluefin tuna.

salmon fish cakes with radish & celery salsa

These are very popular in our home and with my readers. You can make a large batch and keep leftovers for lunch or as a post-workout snack. Salmon provides essential omega-3 fatty acids, while sweet potato is high in beta-carotene and vitamin C.

Preheat the oven to 400°F. Line a small baking sheet with parchment paper.

Place the sweet potato on the prepared baking sheet and bake until soft all the way through, 30 to 40 minutes. Cut in half and let cool.

While the potato is baking, make the salsa: Mix together the radishes, celery, minced green onions, orange juice, lemon juice, horseradish, olive oil, and salt in a small bowl. Set aside.

Bring a pot filled with 1 inch of water to a boil. Add the orange peel and celery leaves. Place the salmon in a colander, then place inside the pot over (but not touching) the water, and cover. (Throw in the peas now if they're frozen.) Steam the fish until light pink and just falling apart, about 4 minutes. (You can also grill the salmon.) Remove from the heat and let cool completely.

Peel the baked potato, put in a large bowl, and mash it roughly with a fork. Remove the skin and bones from the salmon, flake the flesh, and add to the bowl with the mashed potato. Add the peas, chopped green onions, lemon zest, salt, and pepper. Add the egg and tapioca flour and stir gently until well mixed.

In a large frying pan over medium-high heat, warm 2 Tbsp of the ghee. Scoop golf ball–size mounds of the fish mixture into the hot oil, using your fingers to slide the mixture off the spoon. Press and shape the batter into flat, round cakes. Don't overcrowd the pan, and cook in batches as needed. Add the remaining ghee if the pan seems dry. Cook the fish cakes until a golden brown crust forms, about 5 minutes per side.

Serve the fish cakes topped with salsa.

SERVES 2

1 small sweet potato, scrubbed

For the salsa

1½ cup finely chopped radishes

1 celery rib, finely chopped

2 to 3 green onions, minced

2 Tbsp orange juice

2 Tbsp lemon juice

½ tsp horseradish

¼ cup extra-virgin olive oil

½ tsp sea salt

Peel of 1 orange

Leaves of 1 celery rib

2 salmon steaks, about 5 oz each

½ cup frozen or fresh baby peas

½ cup chopped green onions

Zest of 1 lemon

½ tsp sea salt

Pinch of freshly ground black pepper

1 egg, beaten

¼ cup tapioca flour

2 to 3 Tbsp ghee or coconut oil

garlic & saffron poached prawns salad

Inspired by classic Spanish garlic prawns—the ones that sizzle in a clay dish at the table—this recipe uses a poaching method instead of applying high heat to olive oil, which allows it to retain all of its nutrients and delicate flavors and prevents oxidation.

SERVES 2

1½ cups extra-virgin olive oil, plus more for drizzling

5 garlic cloves, thinly sliced

A few threads of saffron

Sea salt

2 vines of cherry tomatoes

1 to 2 Tbsp balsamic vinegar

12 to 14 large prawns

For the salad

2 Tbsp olive oil

½ long red chile, seeded and sliced

Zest and juice of 1 lemon

2 medium zucchini, sliced into thin ribbons

1 Tbsp chopped parsley

Sea salt and freshly ground black pepper

Shaved Parmesan cheese (optional)

Preheat the oven to 350°F.

In a medium saucepan over medium heat, warm the olive oil to 165°F. Add the garlic, saffron, and a pinch of salt and remove from the heat. Set aside to infuse for 30 minutes.

Place the cherry tomatoes, still on the vine, on a rimmed baking sheet and drizzle with olive oil. Roast for 30 minutes. Drizzle with the balsamic vinegar and roast for 10 minutes longer. Set aside. Turn the oven temperature to 175°F.

Peel the prawns, leaving the tails intact, and remove the dark veins. Rinse and set aside.

Place the infused oil over medium heat and bring back to 165°F. Add the prawns to a deep, ovenproof dish and pour the hot oil over them until submerged. Bake, uncovered, for 5 minutes. Flip the prawns and bake until they firm up and turn a light yellow color, 5 to 10 minutes longer.

Meanwhile, make the salad: In a large frying pan over medium heat, warm 1 Tbsp of the olive oil. Throw in the chile, lemon zest, and zucchini ribbons. Toss around for a minute to warm them. Pour the zucchini mixture into a salad bowl. Add the parsley, a pinch each of salt and pepper, the lemon juice, and remaining 1 Tbsp olive oil. Toss in some of the cherry tomatoes and reserve the rest for plating.

Divide the salad among two plates. Using a slotted spoon, gently remove the prawns from the poaching liquid and arrange half on top of each salad. Spoon the reserved roasted tomatoes and some of the soft poached garlic on the side and serve immediately, topped with a few Parmesan shavings, if you like.

chile-chocolate mousse

When I offer this mousse to my guests, I tell them it has no eggs or dairy and I dare them to guess what's in it. "Avocado? No way!" they say in disbelief. "How could something so rich and decadent actually be good for you?" Full of anti-inflammatory nutrients, antioxidants, and healthful fats, this dessert is very easy to whip up, even for the most unexpected dinner party.

SERVES 4

1 large avocado

1½ ripe bananas

6 Tbsp raw cacao powder

3 Tbsp coconut cream

Seeds from ½ vanilla bean

2 Tbsp coconut sugar, raw honey, or maple syrup

Pinch of sea salt

½ tsp red pepper flakes, plus more for garnish

Dark chocolate flakes and/or raspberries for garnish (optional)

Cut the avocado in half and remove the pit. Scoop out the flesh into a food processor or blender. Add the bananas and cacao powder. Process until smooth.

Transfer the avocado mixture to a large bowl and add the coconut cream, vanilla seeds, and coconut sugar. Using a handheld mixer, beat until well combined, fluffy, and smooth. Fold in the salt and red pepper flakes.

You can serve immediately, but it's best to refrigerate the mousse to set for 1 hour. Garnish with dark chocolate flakes, raspberries, and/or a little extra sprinkle of red pepper flakes, as you like.

> Raw cacao powder has more antioxidants than blueberries, red wine, or green tea. You can replace raw cacao powder with melted dark chocolate and, if looking for a lower-carbohydrate version, replace some of the banana with extra avocado and coconut cream.

macadamia cakies

These look and taste like macadamia cookies, but the texture is a little more moist and soft due to almond meal. Basically, they're little cakes pretending to be cookies. No point in calling them what they're not, so from now on they shall be known as "cakies."

MAKES 12 TO 15 CAKIES

⅔ cup raw macadamia nuts

2 eggs, beaten

5 Tbsp coconut oil, melted

3 Tbsp raw honey

1 Tbsp vanilla extract

1½ cups almond meal

2½ Tbsp tapioca flour

1 tsp ground cinnamon

Pinch of sea salt

½ tsp gluten-free baking powder

Preheat the oven to 350°F. Line a baking sheet with two layers of parchment paper.

Coarsely chop the macadamia nuts, or place them in a plastic bag and whack them into smaller pieces with a rolling pin. Transfer to a bowl and set aside.

In a large bowl, combine the eggs, melted coconut oil, honey, and vanilla. Add the almond meal, tapioca, cinnamon, and salt and sprinkle in the baking powder. Fold until everything is well incorporated. Add about three-fourths of the macadamia nuts to the mixture and stir. Refrigerate for 5 minutes.

Make a piping bag out of parchment paper, or snip off one of the bottom corners of a sandwich bag. Scoop the batter into the piping bag.

Squeeze walnut-size dollops of the batter, about ¾ inch apart, onto the prepared baking sheet. Press the remaining nuts gently on top of the cakies and use your fingers or a spatula to gently flatten them.

Bake for 15 minutes. Let cool for 5 to 10 minutes. Store in an airtight container in a cool place for up to 4 days.

raspberry & honey chocolate torte

Full of antioxidants—found in raw cacao and fresh raspberries—and the healthful saturated fat of coconut oil, you won't feel guilty indulging in this scrumptious chocolate cake. It does have a fair amount of almond meal, which is on the higher end of omega-6 fatty acids content, as well as honey, so leave it for special occasions. Serve with a generous side of coconut cream or whipped cream, if you like.

SERVES 10

Melted coconut oil for greasing, plus ¾ cup

½ cup raw cacao powder

¾ cup raw honey

2 Tbsp port or dry sherry

½ cup water

4 eggs, separated

2 cups almond meal

½ cup raspberries, plus more for topping

1 tsp gluten-free baking powder

Pinch of sea salt

Unsweetened shredded coconut for topping

You can replace raw cacao powder with melted dark chocolate and use green-leaf stevia or coconut syrup instead of honey, just adjust the amount based on the concentration of the sweetener.

Preheat the oven to 350°F. Brush a 9-inch round cake pan with melted coconut oil and line the bottom and sides with parchment paper.

In a medium bowl, whisk the cacao powder, honey, ¾ cup coconut oil, port, and water until incorporated.

In a separate bowl, whisk the egg yolks until thick and glossy, 3 to 4 minutes. Fold in the chocolate mixture, the almond meal, and ½ cup raspberries. Sift or sprinkle the baking powder over the mixture evenly.

In a clean, dry bowl, use a handheld mixer to whisk the egg whites with the salt until soft peaks form. Fold some of the egg whites into the chocolate mixture to lighten it, then gently fold in remaining egg whites until just combined.

Pour the mixture into the prepared cake pan. Bake until a skewer inserted into the center comes out clean, about 40 minutes. Let cool completely in the pan.

Transfer the cake to a serving plate and top with raspberries and shredded coconut. Cut into wedges and serve.

ricotta cheesecake with roasted peaches

If heaven exists and it's up in the clouds, this is the cake they serve for afternoon tea. It's fluffy and light with the flavors of tangy, juicy peaches peeking through like rays of sunshine. This cheesecake is high in protein, calcium, and vitamin C; and ricotta is a cheese primarily made from whey, which is less problematic than cheeses that contain mostly casein protein. However, if you're avoiding all dairy, you'll have to sit this one out. More for me!

SERVES 8

Melted coconut oil for greasing

2½ cups fresh ricotta cheese

7 Tbsp green-leaf stevia powder

1 Tbsp tapioca flour

1 tsp vanilla extract

4 eggs, separated

5 Tbsp coconut cream

3 to 4 large ripe peaches

1 to 2 Tbsp coconut sugar

1 Tbsp ground cinnamon

Berries and basil leaves for garnish

You can use a different type of sweetener instead of stevia, such as coconut syrup or honey, although it might change the color of the cake. Any other fruit can be used instead of peaches—fresh berries, kiwifruit, mango, and even fresh figs drizzled with a little honey and lemon.

Arrange one rack in the center of the oven and a second rack in the lower third. Preheat the oven to 325°F. Grease a 9-inch round cake pan with melted coconut oil and line the bottom and sides with parchment paper.

In a large bowl, beat together the ricotta, stevia, tapioca, vanilla, egg yolks, and coconut cream until well blended. In a separate large bowl, beat the egg whites until stiff peaks form. Fold the whites into the ricotta mixture, then pour into the prepared cake pan. Bake on the center rack until golden brown on top, 50 to 60 minutes.

Meanwhile, remove the pits from the peaches and cut the peaches into wedges. Grease a baking sheet with melted coconut oil and line with parchment paper. Arrange the peaches on the baking sheet and sprinkle with the coconut sugar and cinnamon. Roast the peaches on the lower rack of the oven for about 30 minutes.

Transfer the cake to a wire rack and let cool; it will sink slightly. Move the peaches to the center rack and turn the oven temperature to 425°F. Roast the peaches until browned and caramelized, about 10 minutes longer. Let cool.

Starting in the middle, arrange the roasted peaches on top of the cheesecake in a spiral shape. Garnish with a few berries and basil leaves. Store leftovers, covered and refrigerated, for up to 3 days.

mango & blackberry meringue roulade

Take awesome stuff and roll it inside more awesome stuff and this is what you get. My paleo take on the classic meringue roulade was a real crowd-pleaser the first time I served it. It's easy to make, and the best part is you can really play with the fillings. How about strawberries and melted dark chocolate or peaches and toasted almonds with amaretto whisked into the cream?

SERVES 6

For the meringue

Melted coconut oil for greasing

5 egg whites

Pinch of sea salt

6 tsp green-leaf stevia powder

2 tsp tapioca flour

2 tsp white wine vinegar or apple cider vinegar

1 tsp vanilla extract

½ cup unsweetened shredded coconut

1½ cups coconut cream

½ cup heavy cream

2 to 3 tsp green-leaf stevia powder or other natural sweetener

1 mango, peeled, pitted, and diced

1 cup blackberries

To make the meringue: Preheat the oven to 325°F. Grease a baking sheet with melted coconut oil and line with parchment paper.

In a large bowl, beat the egg whites with the salt until soft peaks form. Beat in the stevia, 1 tsp at a time, until well incorporated. Add the tapioca, vinegar, and vanilla and beat until incorporated.

Spoon the egg white mixture onto the prepared baking sheet. Spread in an even layer and smooth the top. Try to maintain a rectangular shape that will readily roll lengthwise into a log. Bake until light golden and firm, 20 to 25 minutes. Transfer to a wire rack and let cool completely. Leave the oven on.

Spread the shredded coconut on a baking sheet and toast in the oven, stirring once, until golden brown, about 2 minutes. Let cool completely. In a medium bowl, whisk together the coconut cream, heavy cream, and stevia.

Flip the meringue onto a clean piece of parchment. Carefully pull away the used paper and discard. Spread the coconut cream mixture over the surface of the meringue, keeping it close to the middle. Top the cream evenly with half of the mango, blackberries, and toasted coconut. Roll up the roulade lengthwise, using the parchment to help. Secure with plastic wrap and refrigerate until set and well chilled, 30 to 60 minutes. Serve sprinkled with the remaining coconut, mango, and berries.

banana muffins with strawberry butter

Believe me when I say that these taste and smell more delicious than what you're imagining in your head right now. The muffins will last a few days, and make an easy addition to kids' lunchboxes. You can use normal butter but my super-easy strawberry version is to die for, and really adds that little bit of decadence to the treat.

MAKES 12 MUFFINS

Coconut oil or olive oil for greasing (optional)

1 cup almond meal

½ cup coconut flour

½ cup tapioca flour

2 tsp gluten-free baking powder

¼ tsp baking soda

1½ ripe bananas, mashed, plus ½ banana, sliced

1 egg

½ cup coconut milk

3 Tbsp raw honey

Seeds of ½ vanilla bean

1 tsp ground cinnamon

Pinch of freshly grated nutmeg

½ cup Strawberry Butter (see page 194)

Preheat the oven to 400°F. Grease a standard 12-well muffin pan with coconut oil or line with paper baking cups.

In a large bowl, whisk together the almond meal, coconut flour, tapioca, baking powder, and baking soda until well incorporated. Add the mashed bananas, egg, coconut milk, honey, vanilla seeds, cinnamon, and nutmeg and blend using a handheld mixer. Fold in the sliced banana.

Divide the mixture among the muffin wells. Bake until raised and brown on the top, 15 to 17 minutes. Serve warm or at room temperature with the strawberry butter.

This recipe can be made without the eggs; just add a little more coconut milk instead. These will keep well in an airtight container, or you can wrap them individually in plastic wrap and refrigerate for lunches and afternoon snacks.

blood orange & strawberry granita

Granita is a semi-frozen Italian dessert that can easily be made at home. Once you know the basic method and ratios, you can create new flavor combinations using freshly squeezed fruit juices, infused teas, and coffee, with coconut milk for creaminess. You can even make savory versions with tomato, carrot, and beet juices.

SERVES 3 OR 4

Juice of 3 blood oranges, zest of 1 blood orange, plus 1 blood orange, sliced

10 strawberries, stemmed, plus more for garnish

1¼ cups water

Juice of ½ lime

1 Tbsp green-leaf stevia powder

¼ tsp vanilla extract

In a medium saucepan over medium-high heat, bring the orange juice, orange zest, strawberries, water, lime juice, stevia, and vanilla to a boil. Simmer for 2 to 3 minutes, remove from the heat, and let cool to room temperature.

In a blender, process the orange mixture until smooth. Pour into a shallow pan, cover with plastic wrap, and freeze until solid.

Remove from the freezer and thaw just a little, then scrape and break up the ice with a fork into a fairly even mixture of ice shards and grains and slush. Scoop into glasses. Garnish with strawberries and blood orange slices and serve immediately.

Other granita combinations:

Apple juice, lime juice, and mint

Amaretto and lemon juice

Tomato, lemon juice, freshly ground black pepper, and sea salt

Blueberres, beet juice, and basil

Carrot juice, ginger, lemon juice, and honey

Coffee, vanilla, and maple syrup

double-decker lamingtons

This is a paleo-friendly version of a classic Australian lamington. These look, smell, and taste like the real thing, except that the texture is little denser and more moist, rather than fluffy and dry.

MAKES 16 SQUARES

For the sponge cake

Olive oil for greasing

A scant ⅔ cup coconut oil

¼ cup raw honey or 2½ Tbsp green-leaf stevia powder

1 tsp vanilla extract

3 eggs

1 tsp gluten-free baking powder or baking soda

½ cup tapioca flour

⅔ cup almond meal

For the chocolate icing

⅔ cup coconut oil

½ cup raw cacao powder

3 Tbsp coconut or almond milk

2 Tbsp pure maple syrup or 1 Tbsp green-leaf stevia powder

1 tsp vanilla extract

1½ cups shredded coconut

To make the cake: Preheat the oven to 325°F. Grease an 8-by-12-inch baking pan with olive oil. Line with parchment paper.

In a medium saucepan over medium heat, melt the coconut oil with the honey and vanilla. Whisk until incorporated.

In a medium bowl, using a handheld mixer, beat the eggs until thick and foamy, about 5 minutes. Gradually add the coconut oil mixture, beating constantly. Add the baking powder, tapioca, and almond meal. Using a whisk or a spatula, fold for 10 to 15 seconds, until incorporated.

Pour the batter into the prepared pan. Bake until a skewer inserted into the center comes out clean, about 20 minutes. Turn the cake onto a wire rack and let cool completely. Trim the edges and cut into four equal strips.

To make the icing: In a medium bowl, combine the coconut oil, cacao powder, coconut milk, maple syrup, and vanilla. Whisk for 1 minute.

Spread the shredded coconut on a plate.

Spread a thin layer of the icing on one side of the cake strips. Stack together two strips, chocolate-sides in. Cut the strips into squares.

Using two forks, dip and coat the pieces with a thin layer of the icing and then dip and roll them in the coconut. Set aside on a wire rack for 1 to 2 hours to set. (If the icing solidifies while you're still working, add 1 to 2 Tbsp of hot water and whisk.)

Store, covered and at room temperature, for up to 1 week.

cherry macaroons

There are the French kind of macarons: glossy, perfectly shaped almond cookies with exquisite creamy filling. Then there are macaroons: chewy, rough-around-the-edges coconut domes many of us associate with childhood trips to the local bakery. Both are made with a base of egg whites and both are very tasty, but one of them follows a complex recipe with multiple processes that requires time, patience, and a bit of skill. This is the easy option!

MAKES 16 MACAROONS

Olive oil for greasing

3 egg whites

Pinch of sea salt

Pinch of cream of tartar

A few drops of white vinegar

2 Tbsp coconut syrup or other natural sweetener

1 tsp rosewater

½ cup almond meal

1½ cups unsweetened shredded coconut

¾ cup pitted cherries, roughly chopped

Preheat the oven to 350°F. Grease a baking sheet with olive oil and line with parchment paper.

In a large bowl, using a handheld mixer, beat the egg whites with the salt until soft peaks form, then add the cream of tartar, vinegar, coconut syrup, and rosewater and beat until stiff and glossy. Fold in the almond meal, shredded coconut, and cherries.

Using a teaspoon and your finger, scoop walnut-size dollops of the batter onto the prepared baking sheet, spacing them about ½ inch apart. Bake until raised and golden brown, 15 to 17 minutes. Let cool before serving.

Cream of tartar, a by-product of winemaking, is also known as potassium hydrogen tartrate. It's an acidic white powder used in conjunction with baking soda as a leavening agent in baking or to increase the stability and volume of beaten egg whites. You can use fresh or canned pitted cherries. Look for unsweetened varieties. Rosewater can be omitted if you don't like the rose-petal flavor, even just a hint.

spiced stewed rhubarb

This is a quick and easy dessert packed with vitamin C and calcium from the pineapple, rhubarb, and yogurt. Those avoiding dairy can serve the rhubarb with nuts and some coconut cream or coconut yogurt.

SERVES 4 OR 5

2½ cups diced rhubarb

⅔ cup diced ripe pineapple

Juice of 1 orange

½ tsp Chinese five-spice powder

2 Tbsp raw honey

2 Tbsp water

½ cup whole Greek yogurt

¼ cup slivered almonds, toasted

In a medium saucepan over medium heat, combine the rhubarb, pineapple, orange juice, five-spice powder, honey, and water. Bring to a simmer and turn the heat to low. Cook until the rhubarb is soft, 10 to 15 minutes.

Serve warm topped with the yogurt and almonds.

jaffa rum balls

These wickedly delicious rum balls are a perfect little treat minus the guilt. They're great to keep on hand as a quick energy snack or to pack as part of your lunch. They are also super-easy to make—there's absolutely no cooking involved—and your kids can help roll the balls.

MAKES 20 BALLS

1 cup almond or hazelnut meal

3 Tbsp raw cacao powder, plus more for dusting

2 Tbsp dark rum

¼ cup plus 2 Tbsp coconut oil

2 Tbsp pure maple syrup or raw honey

½ cup raisins

Zest of 2 oranges

½ cup shredded coconut, plus more for dusting

In a food processor, combine the almond meal, cacao powder, rum, coconut oil, maple syrup, raisins, orange zest, and shredded coconut. Process into a thick mixture. It should come off the sides of the work bowl and form a ball.

Using your fingers, roll the mixture into 20 golf ball–size balls. Dust the finished balls with shredded coconut and cacao powder. Place on a plate and cover with plastic wrap. Store, refrigerated, for up to 3 days.

no-bake energy balls

MAKES 8 TO 10 BALLS

½ cup almonds

½ cup brazil nuts

½ cup sunflower seeds

2 cups water

1 Tbsp lemon juice, plus 1 tsp lemon zest

1 tsp vanilla extract

6 dates, chopped

1½ Tbsp raw cacao powder

1½ Tbsp raw honey

2 Tbsp coconut oil

1 Tbsp chia seeds

In a medium saucepan, cover the almonds, brazil nuts, and sunflower seeds with the water. Add the lemon juice and soak for 4 to 6 hours. This will remove some of the phytic acid and activate the nuts, making them easier to digest. Rinse well and remove the skins from the almonds.

In a food processor, combine the nuts, lemon zest, vanilla, dates, cacao powder, honey, and coconut oil. Process into a thick mixture. Transfer to a medium bowl and mix in the chia seeds. Roll 1-Tbsp-size lumps of dough into balls. Transfer to an airtight container and refrigerate for about 2 hours to set.

Store, refrigerated, for up to 1 week.

kedgeree deviled eggs

This recipe is inspired by kedgeree, a traditional British breakfast from colonial India. It's usually made with rice, smoked fish, boiled eggs, curry powder, and herbs. I took away the rice and came up with these little beauties.

MAKES 12 DEVILED EGGS

6 eggs

6 oz smoked trout

3 Tbsp coconut oil

1 tsp ghee

½ yellow onion, chopped

1 tsp curry powder

1 Tbsp lemon juice

2 Tbsp mayonnaise

Sea salt and freshly ground pepper

Minced dill

You can purchase a whole smoked trout from most fishmongers and supermarkets. Use trout leftovers in a salad, with scrambled eggs or in a celery root remoulade. Covered with plastic wrap or packed in an airtight container, deviled eggs will keep in the fridge for a few days. They make a good addition to a lunchbox or midday snack.

Bring a medium saucepan of water to a rapid boil. Gently lower the eggs into the water and swirl them around gently so that the yolks don't set too close to one side of the shell. Cook for 10 to 12 minutes. Drain and submerge in cold water.

Peel the skin from the trout and pick out the bones. In a small frying pan over medium heat, melt the coconut oil. Add the trout, breaking it into small pieces, and cook until very crisp and golden, 5 to 7 minutes. Drain on a paper towel–lined plate.

In a medium frying pan over medium heat, melt the ghee. Add the onion and sauté until softened and golden, about 8 minutes. Add the curry powder and stir. Transfer to a large bowl.

Peel the hard-boiled eggs. Cut in half lengthwise and remove the yolks. Set the whites aside and put the yolks in the bowl with the onion mixture. Add 2 Tbsp of the fried trout, the lemon juice, 1 tsp of the mayonnaise, and a pinch of salt and pepper.

Fill the egg white halves with the yolk mixture. Top each with a little dollop of mayonnaise, some fried smoked trout, and fresh dill, before serving.

pear & walnut carpaccio

Pear and walnut go beautifully together, especially when served as a semi-savory dish. Pecorino is a cheese made with sheep's milk, and is often a good option for those sensitive to cow's milk. It is completely optional here, but it does add a nice touch of saltiness to balance out the sweetness of the pear.

SERVES 2

2 pears, ripe but not too soft

Juice of ¼ lemon

5 walnuts, plus a few chopped

1 small garlic clove

2 Tbsp macadamia oil or extra-virgin olive oil

1 Tbsp white wine vinegar

Pinch of sea salt

Wild arugula or mustard leaves for serving

Extra-virgin olive oil for drizzling

A few shavings of pecorino romano cheese (optional)

Core the pears and slice into paper-thin slivers. Drizzle and rub them with a little of the lemon juice to prevent browning. Arrange on a large, flat platter, overlapping the slices prettily.

Grind the whole walnuts and garlic in a mortar using a pestle. Add the macadamia oil, vinegar, and salt and stir to mix.

Drizzle the oil mixture over the pears and sprinkle with the chopped walnuts. Pile a handful of arugula on the pears and drizzle with lemon juice and extra-virgin olive oil. Scatter the cheese shavings on top, if desired, and serve.

Wild arugula or mustard leaves have a lovely peppery flavor, but any arugula or green spinach can also be used.

spinach tahini dip

Serve with raw vegetables or as a condiment with seafood or chicken.

MAKES 1 CUP

1 Tbsp extra-virgin olive oil

1 large bunch of spinach, chopped

2 garlic cloves, roughly chopped

2 Tbsp lemon juice

2½ Tbsp tahini

¼ cup macadamia nuts

½ tsp sea salt

Pinch of freshly ground black pepper

In a small saucepan over medium heat, warm the olive oil. Add the spinach and garlic and cook until the spinach is soft and wilted, 1 to 2 minutes. Transfer to a plate and drizzle with the lemon juice.

When cooled, transfer the spinach mixture to a food processor. Add the tahini, macadamia nuts, salt, and pepper and process until smooth. Store, refrigerated, for up to 5 days.

spicy kale chips

Kale chips are the popcorn of the paleo world. Kale is ridiculously nutritious, with lots of iron, calcium, and vitamin C, and it's really easy to make into crispy chips. Make sure to consume kale chips soon after they're ready, as they lose their crispiness quickly. Omit the paprika if you're avoiding nightshades.

SERVES 2

10 large kale leaves

1½ Tbsp extra-virgin olive oil

1 tsp paprika

½ tsp ground coriander

½ tsp ground cumin

1 tsp sea salt

Preheat the oven to 350°F.

Pull the kale leaves off the stems and tough spines and tear or cut with scissors into 1-inch pieces. Wash and dry the leaves in a salad spinner. Toss the clean leaves with the olive oil, paprika, coriander, cumin, and salt.

Scatter the leaves over a large baking sheet and bake for 15 minutes, tossing them every 5 minutes to prevent burning and to make sure they dry out and roast evenly on all sides. The chips will be done in 12 to 15 minutes, depending on your oven, the size of the leaves, and the amount you can fit on your baking sheet. You can bake them in batches, if needed. Serve immediately.

roasted cauliflower bites

SERVES 2 TO 4

3 Tbsp extra-virgin olive oil

2 Tbsp red wine vinegar

2 garlic cloves, minced

½ long red chile, seeded and minced

½ tsp turmeric powder

½ tsp garlic powder

½ tsp paprika

½ tsp ground coriander

1 cauliflower, cut into small florets

Preheat the oven to 350°F.

In a large bowl, combine the olive oil, vinegar, minced garlic, chile, turmeric, garlic powder, paprika, and coriander. Add the cauliflower and toss until well coated. Spread evenly on a baking sheet and bake until lightly browned, 25 to 30 minutes, stirring halfway through. Serve immediately.

prosciutto-wrapped asparagus

MAKES 12 HORS D'OEUVRES

6 very thin slices prosciutto, halved lengthwise

12 asparagus spears, ends trimmed

Ghee for frying

Place a strip of prosciutto on a cutting board, with a short side facing you. Place an asparagus spear on top, at a 45-degree angle to the prosciutto, lining up the end of the asparagus with the bottom left corner of the prosciutto strip. Roll the asparagus in the prosciutto. Repeat with the remaining prosciutto and asparagus. Don't worry if parts of the asparagus spears are not covered completely.

In a large, flat frying pan over medium-high heat, melt enough ghee to coat the bottom of the pan. Add the asparagus and fry until the prosciutto is brown and crispy, 1 to 2 minutes on each side. Serve immediately.

smoky oyster mushrooms

These oyster mushrooms (pictured opposite) are meaty and have a gorgeous umami flavor (which basically means they taste amazing). Eat as chips or use to top salads, stews, and vegetables.

SERVES 2

5 oz oyster mushrooms, brushed clean and broken into quarters

2 Tbsp extra-virgin olive oil

½ tsp garlic powder

½ tsp ground cumin

½ tsp smoked paprika

Good pinch of sea salt

Preheat the oven to 350°F.

In a medium bowl, toss the mushrooms with the olive oil, garlic powder, cumin, paprika, and salt. Spread on a baking sheet. Bake until the mushrooms have crisped and browned, 20 to 25 minutes. Serve immediately.

celery root remoulade & rare roast beef rolls

These are really easy to make and can be served as a starter or packed in a lunchbox. Rare roast beef can be purchased in most good delis.

MAKES 6 ROLLS

½ celery root, peeled and sliced into matchsticks

2 Tbsp chopped green onion

1 tsp horseradish

1 Tbsp mayonnaise

1 Tbsp lemon juice

1 Tbsp chopped parsley

Pinch of freshly ground black pepper

6 slices rare roast beef

In a large bowl, combine the celery root with the green onion, horseradish, mayonnaise, lemon juice, parsley, and pepper. Place equal amounts of the celery root mixture on the lower third of the beef slices and roll tightly upward. Secure with a toothpick if needed and serve immediately.

grilled halloumi with orange-vanilla sauce

If you can tolerate a little dairy, especially goat's and sheep's milk, you will love the balance of salty, sweet, and subtly sour flavors in this dish (pictured opposite). Halloumi cheese is always in our refrigerator and this is a lovely way to serve it for a special party.

SERVES 3 OR 4

Juice of 2 oranges, plus zest of 1 orange removed in large strips

½ vanilla bean, sliced lengthwise

1 Tbsp lemon juice

½ tsp raw honey

Ghee or coconut oil for frying

9 oz halloumi cheese, sliced

Orange slices, mint leaves, and raw pistachios for serving

In a medium saucepan over medium heat, combine the orange juice, orange zest, vanilla bean, lemon juice, and honey and bring to a simmer. Cook until thickened and syrupy, 15 minutes. Remove the orange zest, slice thinly, and set aside. Discard the vanilla bean.

In a large frying pan over high heat, melt enough ghee to cover the bottom of the pan. Add the halloumi and fry until crispy and golden brown, 1 to 2 minutes per side.

Arrange orange slices around the edge of a serving platter and pile the halloumi in the center. Scatter the candied orange zest, mint, and pistachios on top and drizzle with the orange sauce. Serve immediately.

red chile & lime almonds

MAKES 2 CUPS

2 cups raw almonds

1 tsp coconut oil

½ tsp red pepper flakes or chopped fresh red chile

1 small garlic clove, minced

5 lime leaves, minced

Zest of 1 lime, plus 2 Tbsp lime juice

1 Tbsp wheat-free soy sauce

½ tsp sea salt

In a large frying pan over medium heat, toast the almonds, stirring very frequently to prevent burning, until lightly browned and smoky, 15 minutes. Transfer to a plate and set aside.

Add the coconut oil, red pepper flakes, garlic, and lime leaves to the pan. Cook over medium heat, stirring, for about 30 seconds. Add the toasted almonds along with the lime zest, lime juice, soy sauce, and salt. Cook for another minute or two, stirring, to allow the flavors to blend and the almonds to get nicely coated. Serve immediately, or let cool completely and store in an airtight container at room temperature for up to 3 days.

spicy sweet potato fries

Blink and they'll be gone, especially if you have kids hanging around. These fries (pictured opposite) are so much tastier than deep-fried white potato fries—plus, you'll be getting plenty of beta-carotene and vitamin C.

SERVES 4

2 sweet potatoes

¼ cup extra-virgin olive oil

1 tsp paprika

1 tsp ground cumin

1 tsp garlic powder

Sea salt

Pinch of red pepper flakes

Preheat the oven to 375°F. Line two baking sheets with parchment paper.

Peel and cut the sweet potatoes into fries about ¼ inch wide and put in a bowl. Add the olive oil, paprika, cumin, garlic powder, and ½ tsp salt and toss to coat well.

Divide the fries among the prepared baking sheets. Bake until crispy and golden brown, about 30 minutes. Rotate the sheets to ensure even temperature and flip some of the browner fries halfway through baking. Sprinkle with a little more salt and the red pepper flakes and serve immediately.

spicy coconut shrimp

SERVES 6

20 medium-to-large shrimp

¼ cup tapioca flour

2 eggs

1 cup unsweetened shredded coconut

1 tsp onion powder

1 tsp garlic powder

½ tsp chili powder

½ tsp Chinese five-spice powder

1 tsp sea salt

½ cup coconut oil or macadamia oil

Fresh lime wedges or South Eastern Express marinade (see page 198) for serving

Peel the shrimp, leaving the tails intact. Cut out the thick center vein and discard.

Place the tapioca flour in a medium bowl. In a second bowl, whisk the eggs. In a third medium bowl, combine the shredded coconut, onion powder, garlic powder, chili powder, five-spice powder, and salt.

In a deep frying pan or wok over medium-high heat, warm the coconut oil. Dip each shrimp into the flour, shaking off the excess. Dip into the egg, then the coconut mixture.

Add the shrimp to the frying pan in batches and cook until golden, about 2 minutes per side. Don't overcrowd the pan. Transfer the cooked shrimp to a paper towel–lined plate. Serve immediately with lime wedges or with the marinade for dipping.

pickled onion & tomato salad with pancetta

This vitamin C-packed salad is a little beauty. Make it as part of an antipasto platter or as a main side dish with grilled steak or fish. It reminds me of the food my grandmother used to make: lots of pickled vegetables, spices, and strong flavors.

SERVES 3 OR 4

½ tsp coriander seeds

¼ tsp peppercorns

2 Tbsp extra-virgin olive oil

2 Tbsp red wine vinegar

1 tsp mustard seeds

¾ tsp sea salt

1 red onion, thinly sliced into whole rings

Ghee or coconut oil for cooking

4 slices pancetta

2 cups cherry tomatoes, halved

Using a mortar and pestle, grind the coriander seeds and peppercorns into powder. In a large bowl, combine the ground coriander mixture with the olive oil, vinegar, mustard seeds, and salt and stir well. Mix in the onion rings and set aside for at least 20 minutes or up to 1 hour.

In a medium frying pan over medium heat, warm enough ghee to cover the bottom of the pan. Add the pancetta slices and fry until crispy on both sides, about 5 minutes.

Put the tomatoes in a bowl and toss in the pickled onion. Add the crispy pancetta and serve.

You can use ground coriander seed and pepper instead of grinding the seeds and peppercorns. Prosciutto and even bacon can be used instead of pancetta.

tahini crackers

MAKES 12 TO 15 CRACKERS

Soft butter, ghee, or coconut oil
for greasing, plus 1 Tbsp

3 Tbsp tahini

1 egg

2 Tbsp sesame seeds

1 Tbsp grainy mustard

Pinch of sea salt

2½ Tbsp coconut flour

Preheat the oven to 350°F. Lightly grease a sheet of parchment paper with butter.

In a medium bowl, combine the tahini, egg, sesame seeds, 1 Tbsp butter, mustard, and salt and stir until well mixed. Add the coconut flour and stir until a thick, sticky dough forms. (Coconut flour absorbs lots of moisture and so is used sparingly here; you will need to increase the amount if using a different flour.)

Roll the mixture into a ball and place on the prepared parchment. Using your hands, flatten the dough into a pancake shape. Cover with another piece of parchment and use a rolling pin to flatten into a thin round about ⅛-inch thick, starting from the middle and rolling evenly in four directions. Remove the top piece of parchment and use a knife to score the crackers, to make it easier to break apart when baked.

Leaving the dough on the parchment paper, transfer to a baking sheet. Bake for 12 to 15 minutes. When the outer edges start to turn golden brown, remove the baking sheet from the oven, detach the outer crackers, and place them carefully on a wire rack to cool. Return the rest to the oven and bake until lightly golden, 4 to 5 minutes longer.

Let cool before separating into individual crackers. Store in an airtight container at room temperature for up to 6 days.

asian shrimp & pork rolls

MAKES 12 ROLLS

1 Tbsp coconut oil

3 shallots, minced

1 tsp peeled and grated ginger

½ long red chile, seeded and diced

½ lb ground pork

5 shiitake mushrooms (fresh or dried), chopped

1 Tbsp fish sauce

1 Tbsp lime juice

2 tsp coconut aminos

1 garlic clove, minced

1 head napa cabbage, leaves separated

12 cooked and peeled shrimp, halved

Handful of mint leaves

Handful of cilantro leaves

1 large carrot, grated

Asian Twang dressing (see page 196) for serving

In a wok or a frying pan over medium-high heat, melt the coconut oil. Add the shallots, ginger, and chile and cook until softened, about 5 minutes. Add the pork and mushrooms and cook until the meat is slightly browned. Add the fish sauce, lime juice, coconut aminos, and garlic and cook, stirring, until the pork is fully cooked with no more pink showing, about 7 minutes. Set aside.

Meanwhile, bring a large saucepan of water to a boil. Wash 12 good-size cabbage leaves and blanch in the boiling water for about 1 minute. Rinse under cold water to stop the cooking. Pat dry with a clean kitchen towel and trim off the thicker part of the leaf at the bottom.

Place 1 Tbsp of the pork filling in the center of each leaf. Top with 2 shrimp halves, a few mint and cilantro leaves, and a little grated carrot. Fold both sides of the leaf inward and roll up into a tight roll. Serve with the dressing as a dipping sauce.

If using dried shiitake mushrooms, soak them in warm water for 10 minutes to rehydrate before frying. You can use a little palm sugar and gluten-free soy sauce instead of coconut aminos. Normal white cabbage leaves can also be used; however, they should be blanched for a little bit longer. You could also use fresh romaine and make smaller rolls. Omit the chile if avoiding nightshades.

cashew hummus

Blanched almonds or cauliflower can be substituted for the cashews.

MAKES ABOUT 1 CUP

1½ cups cashews

6 tsp lemon juice or white wine vinegar

2 Tbsp tahini

2 Tbsp extra-virgin olive oil

1 garlic clove

½ tsp sea salt

Pinch of freshly ground black pepper

Soak the cashews in warm water and 1 tsp of the lemon juice for 6 hours. Rinse well and transfer to a food processor. Add the remaining 5 tsp lemon juice, ½ cup cool water, the tahini, olive oil, garlic, salt, and pepper and process for 3 to 4 minutes, until very smooth and thick, scraping the sides of the work bowl as you go. Add extra water if needed to get a thinner consistency. Store, refrigerated, for up to 1 week.

lemony harissa

This recipe is the result of multiple experiments with different harissas. It's rich and spicy; and a match made in heaven when drizzled over grilled lamb.

MAKES ABOUT 1 CUP

2 tsp coriander seeds

2 tsp cumin seeds

1 tsp fennel seeds

½ cup extra-virgin olive oil

1 long red chile, seeded and diced

Zest and juice of ½ lemon

¼ preserved lemon, chopped

1 Tbsp chopped cilantro

2 tsp tomato paste

½ tsp caraway seeds

½ tsp smoked paprika, or to taste

Sea salt

½ tsp coconut syrup or raw honey

Using a mortar and pestle or a food processor, grind the coriander seeds, cumin seeds, and fennel seeds into a rough powder. Transfer to a food processor (if necessary) and add the olive oil, ¼ cup water, the chile, lemon zest, lemon juice, preserved lemon, cilantro, tomato paste, caraway seeds, paprika, ½ tsp salt, and coconut syrup. Process to a smooth paste. Taste and add more salt or paprika, if desired. Store, refrigerated, for up to 2 weeks.

> Lemony harissa can be used to marinate lamb, beef, or chicken or used on top of grilled seafood. It can also be added to stews and African tagines.

roasted tomato ketchupy sauce

I had been looking for a good recipe for tomato sauce/tomato ketchup that didn't use added sugar and wasn't flavored with enhancers or other nasty additives. After a few experiments, this is what I came up with. It's inspired by a few different methods and my own little twists. I use carrots and roasted tomatoes, both of which caramelize and provide sweetness during cooking.

MAKES ABOUT 1 PINT

1 lb ripe plum tomatoes

Extra-virgin olive oil for drizzling, plus 3 Tbsp

Sea salt

1 yellow onion, minced

1 rib celery, minced

2 carrots, finely grated

1 thumb-size nub of ginger, peeled and finely grated

2 garlic cloves, minced

½ red chile, seeded and minced

1 Tbsp minced oregano

1 Tbsp coriander seeds

1 tsp smoked paprika

1 tsp fish sauce

3 cloves

2 bay leaves

1 tsp freshly ground black pepper

1½ cups canned tomatoes, drained and diced

½ cup red wine vinegar, or to taste

1 cup water

Preheat the oven to 350°F. Line a baking sheet with aluminum foil.

Pile the plum tomatoes on the prepared baking sheet. Drizzle with olive oil and sprinkle with 1 tsp salt. Roast for 30 minutes. Remove from the oven and set aside.

In a heavy-bottomed medium saucepan over low heat, warm 3 Tbsp olive oil. Add the onion, celery, and carrots and cook, stirring occasionally, until softened, about 15 minutes.

Add the ginger, garlic, chile, oregano, coriander seeds, paprika, fish sauce, cloves, bay leaves, 1 tsp salt, and black pepper to the pan. Cook for 1 minute, then add the roasted tomatoes, canned tomatoes, vinegar, and water. Turn the heat to high and bring to a boil. Turn the heat to medium-low and simmer gently until the sauce is reduced by half.

Transfer to a food processor and purée until well blended. Push through a fine-mesh sieve to remove any skin or unblended ingredients. Return to the saucepan, place over low heat, and simmer for 15 minutes to thicken. Taste for seasoning and add more salt or vinegar, if needed. Pour the sauce into sterilized jars or bottles, seal tightly, and refrigerate for up to 3 months.

bone broth

I remember my grandmother had a huuuge pot in which she often boiled a bunch of bones. She would use the gelatin-rich liquid to make holodetz, a traditional dish of soft-cooked meat covered in meat-stock jelly. I loved the taste, but I had no idea how nutritious it was. Today, homemade bone broth is going through a renaissance. Forget about "an apple a day keeps the doctor away"; it's all about a daily cup of bone broth to heal your gut, improve immunity, reduce joint and arthritis pain, and to keep your nails, skin, and hair looking healthy and beautiful.

MAKES ABOUT 3½ QUARTS

5½ lb mixed bones (beef marrow, knuckle bone, and some meatier bones like ribs and neck)

3 to 4 qt cold water

3 Tbsp white wine vinegar

2 yellow onions, quartered

2 large carrots, chopped

2 celery stalks, chopped

1 tsp black peppercorns

1 Tbsp sea salt

3 garlic cloves

1 star anise

Bouquet garni of thyme, bay leaf, and parsley

> Drink bone broth like a soup, use to braise vegetables, or use as a stock base for casseroles, stews, sauces, and gravy.

Preheat the oven to 350°F.

Place the bones with less meat in a tall stockpot. Cover with the water and add the vinegar. (The acidity of the vinegar will help release the nutrients from the bones.) Set aside for 40 minutes. In the meantime, place the meatier bones in a roasting pan and roast until nicely browned, about 40 minutes.

Add the roasted bones to the stockpot, turn the heat to medium-high, and bring to a boil. Some of the impurities will float to the top as grayish foam; skim it off with a slotted spoon.

Add the onions, carrots, celery, peppercorns, and salt to the pot. Return to a boil and then turn the heat to low to maintain a gentle simmer. Cook for about 12 hours. Check every 20 minutes for the first hour or two to remove any new scum that floats to the top. Add the garlic, star anise, and bouquet garni for the last 2 hours of cooking.

Remove the bones with tongs or a slotted spoon. Strain the broth into a large container or bowl. Refrigerate to cool and then use a spoon to remove the congealed fat that forms at the top. Transfer to smaller containers; refrigerate for immediate use or freeze for up to 3 months.

red chile dip

This lovely dip (pictured opposite) is full of big flavors. Eat with your favorite crispy vegetables or use as a stuffing for mushrooms and meatballs.

MAKES ABOUT 1½ CUPS

¾ cup cashews

1 tsp lemon juice or white wine vinegar

½ cup extra-virgin olive oil

10 sun-dried tomatoes, sliced

½ large red bell pepper, seeded and diced

1 long red chile, seeded and diced

2 Tbsp red wine vinegar

1 Tbsp tomato paste

1 garlic clove, diced

2 pinches of sea salt

Pinch of freshly ground black pepper

Soak the cashews in warm water to cover and the lemon juice for 6 hours. Drain, rinse well, and transfer to a food processor. Add the olive oil, tomatoes, bell pepper, chile, vinegar, tomato paste, garlic, salt, pepper, and a splash of cool water. Process for 3 to 4 minutes, scraping the sides of the work bowl occasionally, until very smooth and thick. Store, refrigerated, for up to 1 week.

creamy spinach & egg dip

MAKES ABOUT 1½ CUPS

1 bunch spinach

5 hard-boiled eggs, peeled

3 Tbsp mayonnaise

2 Tbsp chopped green onion

1 Tbsp lemon juice

1 garlic clove, minced

½ tsp sea salt

½ tsp freshly ground black pepper

Bring a large saucepan of water to a boil. Add the spinach and blanch for about 30 seconds. Drain and rinse under cold water. Squeeze out and chop roughly. Place in a food processor and add the eggs, mayonnaise, green onion, lemon juice, garlic, salt, and pepper. Purée until smooth. Serve within 2 hours.

homemade coconut yogurt

There is only one thing you need to know about making your own coconut yogurt—it's a lot easier than you think. Once you get the tools and the ingredients, there is really not that much to it. It tastes just like any other natural yogurt, but with a light coconut flavor. Perfect for keeping your gut flora healthy and your morning granola as tasty as ever.

MAKES A GENEROUS 3 CUPS

Two 14-oz cans coconut cream

¾ tsp yogurt-starter culture

Equipment

2 clean glass jars with lids

A saucepan

A small cup and a spoon

A kitchen towel

An instant-read thermometer

Insulated bag

You can purchase yogurt-starter culture in powder form at most health-food stores, usually found in the refrigerated section. You can also use some of your current yogurt as a culture for your next yogurt.

In a large pot of boiling water, sterilize the jars, lids, saucepan, and cup and spoon you will be using for this recipe. Dry on a clean kitchen towel.

Pour the coconut cream into the prepared saucepan, reserving as much of the watery liquid that sinks to the bottom as possible. Gently heat to 110°F. Remove from the heat immediately.

Add 1 Tbsp of the warm coconut cream to a prepared cup. Add the yogurt-starter culture and stir into a thick paste. Add a little more of the warm cream and stir again. Pour the mixture back into the saucepan and stir to mix thoroughly.

Pour the mixture into the prepared jars and seal with the lids. Wrap both jars in the kitchen towel and place in the insulated bag. Essentially you want to maintain the temperature as close to 100°F for as long as possible. (Instead of the insulated bag, you can wrap the jars in aluminum foil and some towels.) Leave in a warm place for 12 hours. Refrigerate for another 12 hours before eating.

garlic jam

MAKES 1½ CUPS

3 cups unpeeled garlic cloves

Olive oil for drizzling

3 Tbsp macadamia oil or ghee

1 yellow onion, sliced

10 sun-dried tomatoes, sliced

1 cup vegetable stock

½ cup coconut syrup or raw honey

Zest and juice of 1 lemon

2 tsp salt

1 tsp red pepper flakes

½ tsp freshly ground black pepper

½ tsp ground coriander

You can make a similar jam with roasted onions or leeks. Use the jam as a condiment with grilled meats and fish, on eggs, or stirred into casseroles and sauces to add some of that beautiful, sweet yet subtle garlic flavor.

Preheat the oven to 350°F.

Spread the garlic cloves in a large roasting pan and drizzle with olive oil to coat well. Roast for 30 minutes. Set aside until cool enough to handle.

Meanwhile, in a medium saucepan over medium heat, warm the macadamia oil. Add the onion and sun-dried tomatoes and cook until the onion is softened, about 7 minutes.

Peel the roasted garlic cloves, trying to keep them intact. Add to the saucepan with the onion and tomatoes. Add the vegetable stock, coconut syrup, lemon zest, lemon juice, salt, red pepper flakes, black pepper, and coriander. Bring to a boil, then turn the heat to medium-low and simmer for 1 hour, stirring a few times. The mixture will thicken and caramelize.

Let cool to room temperature before transferring to sterilized jars. Cover the top with a piece of plastic wrap and an airtight lid. Store, refrigerated, for up to 2 months.

beef jerky

Beef jerky is a popular snack but it can be a little expensive, and you can't always find a brand that uses natural ingredients and grass-fed beef. You can easily make your own using a nice, grass-fed piece of beef. Make sure it's lean, as fatty cuts can go rancid when stored. Go for cuts such as flank steak and London broil.

MAKES 10 TO 12 OZ

1 lb beef fillet, washed and patted dried

2½ tsp sea salt

2 tsp ground coriander

1 tsp smoked paprika

1 tsp garlic powder

1 tsp onion powder

1 tsp freshly ground black pepper

1 tsp red pepper flakes

Place the meat in the freezer for 30 to 60 minutes, until firmed up but not completely hard. Slice it into thin strips.

In a small bowl, combine the salt, coriander, paprika, garlic powder, onion powder, black pepper, and red pepper flakes. Coat the meat strips with the spice mixture. Cover and refrigerate for 12 hours.

Preheat the oven to 175°F. Line the bottom of the oven with aluminum foil.

Lay the meat strips directly on the oven rack so that air can circulate around them. Place the rack in the center of the oven and bake for 3 hours, turning the strips halfway through. Crack the oven door to allow the temperature to lower to 110°F. Leave the door partially open and bake until the jerky is darkened and cracks when bent, 3 to 4 hours. Remove the rack and let the jerky cool completely. Store in an airtight container, refrigerated, for up to 1 month.

purple sauerkraut

Sauerkraut is a staple in Ukrainian cuisine, and I often watched my parents make large batches of fermented cabbage in a bathtub. Yep, that's how much sour cabbage we went through, especially in winter when many fresh vegetables were out of season. Fresh sauerkraut is a fantastic addition to your meals, as the fermentation process develops probiotics essential for a healthy gut. Start with a small batch using this recipe before you attempt a bathtubful.

MAKES 2 TO 3 CUPS

¼ **large head purple or white cabbage**

1 medium carrot, grated

1 garlic clove

1½ Tbsp sea salt

½ tsp ground coriander

Other spices and flavors to add to your sauerkraut include caraway seeds, dill seeds, mustard seeds, celery seeds, juniper berries, onion, pepper, turmeric, and ginger. You can use leftover sauerkraut mixed in with a new batch to kick-start the fermentation process.

Thinly slice or shred the cabbage, discarding the core. In a large bowl, combine the cabbage, carrot, garlic, salt, and coriander. Using your hands, toss to mix well and squeeze the mixture to help release the liquid. Use a meat tenderizer or wooden spoon to pound the mixture for a few minutes to release the juices. Alternatively (this is what I do), place a saucer or a small plate on top of the mixture inside the bowl, cover it with plastic wrap, put a small kettle or other weight on top of the plate, and press it down gently. Let stand for a couple of hours to release more liquid.

Transfer the cabbage to a sterilized medium glass jar, pressing the cabbage down with a spoon or your clean hand to release more juice to the top. Leave a ½-inch space between the top of the jar and the cabbage. Make sure the cabbage is completely covered with brine.

Cover tightly and leave at room temperature for about 3 days. The vegetables will soften and change color slightly; when you open the lid, it should smell acidic and sharp. If any mold forms on the top, just remove it. Serve immediately or store, refrigerated, indefinitely.

cashew satay sauce

Serve satay sauce with chicken, beef, or lamb skewers, or make it into a slightly thinner sauce for Indonesian Gado Gado salad with lots of cooked and raw vegetables, boiled eggs, and fresh herbs.

MAKES 1 CUP

3 small shallots, peeled and chopped

3 small red chiles, seeded

2 garlic cloves, chopped

1 stalk lemongrass, peeled and chopped

2 tsp curry powder

1 tsp turmeric powder

1½ Tbsp coconut oil

3 cups unsalted raw cashews

1½ cups water

¾ cup coconut milk

Juice of ½ lime

2 Tbsp coconut aminos

3 tsp fish sauce

1 Tbsp raw honey

Pinch of sea salt

In a food processor, combine the shallots, chiles, garlic, lemongrass, curry powder, and turmeric powder and process to a smooth paste.

In a large saucepan over medium heat, melt the coconut oil. Add the spice paste and fry for 4 to 5 minutes, stirring frequently to prevent sticking. The mixture will start caramelizing and browning slightly.

Meanwhile, in a medium frying pan over medium heat, toast the cashews for 2 minutes, stirring frequently to prevent burning.

Add 1 cup of the water to the spice paste and bring to a boil. In a clean food processor, grind the toasted cashews into crumbs and add to the spice paste mixture. Add the coconut milk, lime juice, coconut aminos, and fish sauce. Bring to a boil, then lower the heat to bring the mixture to a simmer. Cook for 5 minutes, then add the honey, salt, and remaining ½ cup water. Cook for 5 minutes longer, stirring frequently as the mixture starts thickening. Remove from the heat and transfer to a blender. Blend into a very smooth paste (adding a little more water as needed).

Transfer to a sterilized airtight jar and store, refrigerated, for up to 1 week.

homemade mayo

When I transitioned into paleo, I had a mini panic attack because I thought mayonnaise would be a complete no-no. For me, it's been its own food group for most of my life. Thankfully, it's very much paleo friendly as it is essentially an egg yolk and oil emulsion with some mustard, vinegar, and salt. This recipe is an adaption from Julia Child's method.

Warm a large bowl in hot water and dry it. Add the egg yolks to the warm bowl and, using a handheld mixer, beat until thick and sticky, 1 to 2 minutes. Add the vinegar, salt, and mustard. Beat for 30 seconds longer.

Add the macadamia oil drop by drop, beating constantly until the sauce has thickened. Keep your eye on the oil rather than on the sauce. Stop pouring every 10 seconds or so but continue beating to be sure the egg yolks are absorbing the oil.

After ⅓ to ½ cup of oil has been incorporated, the sauce will thicken into a heavy cream and the potential crisis of curdling is over. Beat in the remaining oil by tablespoons, blending thoroughly after each addition. When the sauce becomes too thick and stiff, beat in drops of vinegar to thin it out. Then continue with the oil.

Finally, beat the boiling water into the sauce. This is an anti-curdling insurance. Season to taste. If the sauce is not used immediately, scrape it into a small bowl and cover it tightly with plastic wrap to prevent a skin forming on its surface. Store, refrigerated, for up to 3 days.

MAKES 2 CUPS

3 egg yolks, at room temperature

1 Tbsp wine vinegar or lemon juice, plus more as needed

½ teaspoon sea salt

½ teaspoon dry or prepared mustard

1½ cups macadamia oil

2 Tbsp boiling water

The maximum amount of oil one egg yolk can absorb is about ¾ cup, after which the binding properties of the egg break down and the sauce starts to thin and curdle. The safest amount is ½ cup of oil per egg yolk. The proportions of ingredients look something like this: 2 egg yolks + 1 cup fat (oil) + 2 to 3 Tbsp vinegar/lemon juice = about 1½ cups mayonnaise.

red curry paste

Having some red curry paste on hand is very useful, as you can toss it in a stir-fry or mix it with some coconut milk for a quick pumpkin or chicken curry. It's also great for marinating meats and seafood. You might have to make a trip to an Asian market for some of these ingredients.

MAKES 1 CUP

3 shallots, diced

4 garlic cloves, roughly chopped

2 long red chiles, seeded and diced

1 stalk lemongrass, peeled and sliced

1½ Tbsp grated galangal

1½ Tbsp grated turmeric root

7 lime leaves

3 cilantro stems, chopped

2 Tbsp extra-virgin olive oil

1½ Tbsp fish sauce

½ tsp grated palm sugar

½ tsp shrimp paste (optional)

Olive oil for storing

In a food processor, combine the shallots, garlic, chiles, lemongrass, galangal, turmeric, lime leaves, cilantro, olive oil, fish sauce, palm sugar, and shrimp paste. Purée into as smooth a paste as possible, 2 to 3 minutes. Store, refrigerated, in an airtight container, covered with a layer of olive oil, for up to 1 week.

three butters

I love butter for its lush texture, its ability to make everything taste better, and its amazing nutritional profile. Even those avoiding dairy can indulge in a little butter, given that it's mostly fat with very few milk solids. These three butters are very versatile in the kitchen and can be kept refrigerated or frozen, ready to smother grilled fish, steak, or a stack of pancakes.

EACH RECIPE MAKES ABOUT ½ CUP

LIME & CILANTRO BUTTER

Use on grilled fish, shrimp, scallops, or chicken; toss with spinach, broccoli, or green peas; or melt over savory muffins and fritters.

3½ oz softened unsalted butter

2 Tbsp chopped cilantro

Zest and juice of 1 lime

½ tsp sea salt

½ tsp freshly ground black pepper

STRAWBERRY BUTTER

Eat by the spoonful, melt over muffins and pancakes, or mix with some puréed cashews or macadamia nuts as a frosting for cupcakes.

3½ oz softend unsalted butter

10 strawberries, stemmed and finely diced

1 tsp vanilla extract

SIMPLE CAFÉ DE PARIS BUTTER

Amazing on grilled red meat, roasts, baked sweet potatoes, roasted asparagus, and mushrooms; use for flavoring meatballs, and for finishing off meat casseroles, sauces, and stews.

3½ oz softened unsalted butter

1 Tbsp gluten-free Worcestershire sauce

1 Tbsp capers, drained

1 garlic clove, chopped

1 tsp Dijon mustard

1 tsp lemon juice

2 anchovies, chopped

½ tsp sea salt

½ tsp freshly ground black pepper

½ tsp curry powder

Leaves of 2 sprigs thyme

Place the butter and flavorings in a food processor and purée until well combined. Refrigerate in a glass or plastic container indefinitely.

beloved salad dressings

These dressings are more like idea starters—I wanted to give you something fun, exotic, maybe a little weird. Rest assured, they are all delicious.

ASIAN TWANG

Use for Asian coleslaw, Thai beef salad, oysters, or over grilled fish. Use as a dipping sauce for chicken wings.

MAKES ⅓ CUP

2 Tbsp extra-virgin olive oil

1½ Tbsp fresh lime juice

1 Tbsp fish sauce

1 Tbsp chopped cilantro

1 small nub of ginger, peeled and chopped

½ small red chile, seeded and chopped

1 tsp sesame oil

½ tsp grated palm sugar

Whisk all the ingredients in a bowl. Store in airtight glass jars, refrigerated, for up to 1 week.

HAZELNUT & VANILLA

Drizzle over roasted pumpkin and carrots, or grilled eggplant. Also perfect over grilled calamari and prawns.

MAKES ⅓ CUP

¼ cup hazelnuts, toasted and chopped

2 Tbsp extra-virgin olive oil

1 Tbsp hazelnut oil

1 Tbsp apple cider vinegar

1 tsp vanilla extract

½ tsp raw honey

½ tsp Dijon mustard

¼ tsp garlic powder

Whisk all the ingredients in a bowl. Store in airtight glass jars, refrigerated, for up to 1 week.

TAHINI & GARLIC

Really good with beet and goat cheese salad, pear salad, green bean salad, or over roasted leeks.

MAKES ⅔ CUP

Zest and juice of 1 lemon

1 Tbsp tahini

1 garlic clove, grated

½ cup extra-virgin olive oil

½ tsp ground cumin

Pinch of sea salt and freshly ground black pepper

Whisk all the ingredients in a bowl. Store in airtight glass jars, refrigerated, for up to 1 week.

TOMATO ZING

MAKES 1 CUP

⅔ cup extra-virgin olive oil

½ cup sun-dried tomatoes

Juice of 2 lemons, plus 1 tsp lemon zest

1 garlic clove

1 tsp Dijon mustard

½ tsp red pepper flakes or chopped chile

½ tsp sea salt

Process all the ingredients in a blender or a food processor until smooth. Store in airtight glass jars, refrigerated, for up to 1 week.

TUTTI FRUTTI

This dressing is great on top of a ceviche or freshly grilled tuna or salmon; and in crispy summer salads with radishes, fennel, arugula, spinach, cherry tomatoes, or cucumbers.

MAKES ⅔ CUP

½ cup extra-virgin olive oil

2 Tbsp orange juice, plus ½ tsp orange zest

1 Tbsp lime juice, plus ½ tsp lime zest

1 Tbsp lemon juice, plus ½ tsp lemon zest

1 Tbsp chopped basil

1 tsp onion powder

1 tsp Dijon mustard

½ tsp sea salt

½ tsp freshly ground black pepper

Whisk all the ingredients in a bowl. Store in airtight glass jars, refrigerated, for up to 1 week.

AVOCADO RANCH

Use this thick dressing for burgers, coleslaw, sweet potato fries, Mexican pulled pork, or paleo pizza sauce; or for dipping grilled prawns, chicken bites, or vegetable crudités.

MAKES ⅔ CUP

1 avocado, pitted, peeled, and mashed

¼ cup water

2 Tbsp mixed chopped chives, parsley, and dill

1 Tbsp coconut cream

1 Tbsp white wine vinegar

1 Tbsp extra-virgin olive oil

1 tsp Dijon mustard

½ tsp onion powder

½ tsp garlic powder

½ tsp sea salt

½ tsp ground white pepper

Process all the ingredients in a blender or a food processor until smooth. Store in airtight glass jars, refrigerated, for up to 1 week.

top-notch marinades

Marinating before cooking infuses flavor and kicks off the process by softening the main ingredient. The recipes below are calculated for about 1 lb of meat.

BRONTE BEACH SUMMERS

Great with red meat and lamb.

½ cup extra-virgin olive oil

2 Tbsp balsamic vinegar

2 Tbsp gluten-free Worcestershire sauce

1 garlic clove, minced

1 tsp sweet paprika

1 tsp sea salt

1 tsp dried Italian herbs or minced parsley

½ tsp freshly ground black pepper

ARABIC NIGHTS

Rub all over lamb, goat, beef, or chicken. It's great with vegetables too—try it on eggplants, carrots, pumpkin, and red bell peppers. Add a spoonful to stews and tagines for a kick.

½ cup extra-virgin olive oil

1 Tbsp lemon juice

¼ preserved lemon, chopped

1 tsp ground cumin

1 tsp ground coriander

1 tsp ground caraway seeds

1 tsp turmeric powder

1 tsp tahini

1 tsp sea salt

SOUTH EASTERN EXPRESS

Make tantalizing chicken wings, beef skewers, or grilled prawns; or drizzle over baked salmon.

2 Tbsp extra-virgin olive oil

1 Tbsp lime juice

1 Tbsp gluten-free soy sauce

1 Tbsp raw honey

1 Tbsp fish sauce

1 tsp sesame oil

1 tsp grated garlic

1 tsp grated ginger

½ tsp red pepper flakes

STICKY PORTUGUESE

Goes well with poultry, red meat, and seafood.

½ red onion, diced

¼ cup extra-virgin olive oil

2 Tbsp red wine vinegar

1 long red chile, seeded and diced

2 garlic cloves, minced

1½ Tbsp tomato paste

1 Tbsp dry sherry or port

1½ tsp smoked paprika

1 tsp sweet paprika

1 tsp raw honey or coconut syrup

1 tsp sea salt

½ tsp ground coriander

Use a food processor to purée the ingredients or whisk in a bowl.

homemade spice mixes

Making your own spice mixes is fun and is the best way to know what's in them.

MOROCCAN

Use for tagines and stews, or to rub on chicken, beef, goat, or fish.

1 tsp ground coriander

1 tsp ground cumin

1 tsp paprika

1 tsp turmeric powder

½ tsp garlic powder

½ tsp onion powder

½ tsp sea salt

½ tsp freshly ground black pepper

INDIAN

Great for grilled meats and seafood, or a spice base for a curry.

2 tsp sweet paprika

1 tsp ground cumin seeds

1 tsp turmeric powder

1 tsp onion powder

½ tsp ground coriander

½ tsp ground cloves

½ tsp ground cinnamon

½ tsp ground cardamom

½ tsp chili powder

MEXICAN FIESTA

Did someone say "tacos"?

1 tsp sweet paprika

1 tsp ground coriander seeds

1 tsp ground cumin seeds

1 tsp dried oregano

½ tsp chili powder

½ tsp sea salt

½ tsp freshly ground black pepper

SZECHUAN SALT MIX

Sprinkle on grilled duck, quail, shrimp, or steak.

2 Tbsp sea salt

1 Tbsp Szechuan peppercorns, finely ground

1 tsp onion powder

½ tsp garlic powder

½ tsp red pepper flakes

CAJUN

Use for ribs, chicken, fish, and steaks.

2 tsp paprika

2 tsp cayenne pepper

2 tsp garlic powder

2 tsp onion powder

2 tsp ground white pepper

1 tsp dried oregano

1 tsp dried thyme

1 tsp sea salt

Mix in a dry bowl. Store in an airtight container for up to 6 months.

cashew raita

MAKES ABOUT 1 CUP

⅔ cup cashews

Juice of 1 lemon or 2 Tbsp white wine vinegar

¾ tsp tahini

1 Tbsp extra-virgin olive oil

½ garlic clove, minced

½ tsp ground cumin

Pinch of sea salt

½ medium cucumber, minced

1 Tbsp chopped mint

Soak the cashews in warm water to cover with the lemon juice for 4 to 6 hours. Drain and rinse well. Add the nuts to a food processor with ½ cup water, the tahini, olive oil, garlic, cumin, and salt. Process until smooth, 3 to 4 minutes.

Transfer the cashew mixture to a small bowl and stir in the cucumber and mint. Store, refrigerated, for up to 1 week.

hot caraway mustard

Mustard is very easy to make and there are many variations, depending on the color of the mustard seeds, the temperature of the water, and the use of other spices and herbs. This mustard is quite spicy, but you can use warm water when mixing to make it more mild. The turmeric adds gorgeous bright color.

MAKES ABOUT 1 CUP

3 Tbsp yellow mustard seeds

½ tsp caraway seeds

½ tsp black peppercorns

2½ Tbsp white wine vinegar

¼ cup white mustard powder

½ tsp turmeric powder

1 tsp sea salt

½ cup warm water (or cold if you like it very hot and spicy)

Using a mortar and pestle or food processor, grind the mustard seeds, caraway seeds, and peppercorns to a coarse powder. Transfer to a bowl and stir in the vinegar, mustard powder, turmeric, salt, and water. Transfer to a glass jar, cover, and refrigerate for 12 hours for the flavors to develop. Store, refrigerated, for up to 4 weeks.

mixed berry & chocolate smoothie

This is dessert in a glass (pictured opposite). Think Black Forest cake or a mixed-berry chocolate pudding. It's rich in protein from whey powder and antioxidants from berries and cacao powder.

SERVES 2

1 cup frozen mixed berries, plus more for garnish

1 cup coconut milk

2 Tbsp whey protein powder

1 tsp raw cacao or cocoa powder

1 tsp sugar-free berry jam

Dark chocolate shavings for sprinkling

In a blender, combine the berries, coconut milk, protein powder, cacao powder, and jam and process until smooth and thick. Add a little water if using chilled coconut milk, which tends to thicken in the refrigerator. Pour into glasses, garnish with a few berries, sprinkle with chocolate shavings, and serve.

aperol spritz

I fell in love with this drink in Italy. It's made with Aperol, an aperitif similar to Campari and made with bitter orange, rhubarb, and licorice, among other ingredients. Serve as a pre-dinner drink to get your taste buds and appetite into gear. My recipe is slightly modified from the original.

SERVES 1

1 lemon slice

1 orange slice, plus 2 Tbsp orange juice

1 oz Aperol

Ice cubes

5 oz prosecco

1 oz soda water

Place the lemon slice and orange slice in the bottom of a glass. Pour in the orange juice and Aperol. Add ice and slowly pour in the prosecco. Stir gently and splash with soda water. Serve immediately.

glory beets

This invigorating juice (pictured opposite) is a great way to start the day. Beets contain powerful antioxidants, lots of iron, and folic acid. Paired with fragrant strawberries, crunchy green apple, and carrots, this is one tasty, nutritious drink. You will need a juicer.

MAKES 1 TO 2 CUPS

2 beets

2 carrots

3 green apples, quartered

5 strawberries

1 celery rib

1 thumb-size nub of ginger (optional)

½ cup ice cubes

Juice all the ingredients in a juicer. Stir and pour into glasses. Serve immediately.

lychee-lemongrass sangria

Summer weekends should feature a chilled jug of sangria. You might be more familiar with red wine sangria, but it's time to try something different. This white wine version is light, fragrant, and exotic.

MAKES ABOUT 4 CUPS

One 750-ml bottle white wine

1 stalk lemongrass, pale part only, peeled and cut in thirds

Zest of 1 lime, plust 2 Tbsp lime juice

1 green apple, cored and diced

1 cup drained canned lychees

½ cup low-sugar grape juice

1 cup soda water

Ice cubes

Handful of mint leaves

In a pitcher, combine the wine, lemongrass, lime zest, lime juice, apple, lychees, and grape juice. Refrigerate overnight. Add the, soda water, ice, and fresh mint before serving.

sunday bloody mary

One of my favorite drinks is a good Bloody Mary, and what makes a Bloody Mary good is the tomato juice mix you use to serve over vodka and ice. It's best and easiest to mix the juice ahead of time to allow the flavors and spices to fuse together. This Bloody Mary mix is what I used during my cocktail-making days. Pour the mixture over ice for a virgin Bloody Mary.

MAKES 1 QUART MIX

For the Bloody Mary mix

4¼ cups good-quality tomato juice, no sugar added

1 Tbsp horseradish

Zest and juice of ½ orange

Zest and juice of ½ lemon

3 Tbsp gluten-free Worcestershire sauce

1 Tbsp Tabasco sauce

1½ Tbsp dry sherry or port

1 tsp fish sauce

½ tsp sea salt

½ tsp freshly ground black pepper

Chile Celery Salt

1 tsp red pepper flakes

1 tsp celery seeds

1 Tbsp sea salt

For each cocktail

1 lemon wedge

Sea salt or Chile Celery Salt (above)

1 celery rib

2 oz good-quality vodka

1 cup ice cubes

⅔ cup Bloody Mary mix (above)

1 cherry tomato

1 green olive

To make the Bloody Mary mix: In a large jar or bottle, combine the tomato juice, horseradish, orange zest, orange juice, lemon zest, lemon juice, Worcestershire, Tabasco, sherry, fish sauce, salt, and black pepper. Shake to mix well. Use right away or store, refrigerated, for up to 3 days.

To make the celery salt: Grind the red pepper flakes, celery seeds, and salt in a mortar and pestle. Store in an airtight container indefinitely.

To make one cocktail: Rub the rim of a tall glass with the lemon wedge and dip it into the salt. Place the celery inside the glass and pour in the vodka. Fill halfway with ice and pour in the Bloody Mary mix to fill. Pierce the cherry tomato and green olive with a cocktail stirrer and put in the glass. Serve immediately.

blueberry dreams

If using frozen blueberries, rinse them under hot water to thaw. Water or apple juice can used instead of coconut water.

MAKES 1 TO 1½ CUPS

½ cup blueberries

½ cup diced mango

½ cup coconut water

½ cup ice cubes

1 Tbsp lemon juice

1 tsp vanilla extract

In a blender, combine the blueberries, mango, coconut water, ice, lemon juice, and vanilla and purée into a smooth, thick drink. Serve immediately.

bimka

Before I became a good cook, I was really good at making cocktails. In fact, for a little while, I used to teach cocktail classes in a high-profile Sydney bar. This was one of the cocktails I made up for the menu at the time. It's named after my first dog, Bimka.

SERVES 1

1½ Tbsp vodka

2 Tbsp apple sour liqueur

¼ cup apple juice

1 Tbsp lime juice

5 blueberries

1 cup ice cubes

1 Tbsp crème de cassis

½ green apple, cored and thinly sliced

In a cocktail shaker, combine the vodka, liqueur, apple juice, and lime juice. Drop the blueberries into a tall cocktail glass and add the ice. Shake the cocktail mixture and pour over the ice. Pour the crème de cassis down the side of the glass, letting it sink to the bottom and creating a gradient in the liquid. Fan the apple slices on top of the drink and serve immediately.

honey-ginger beer

You need dry yeast to make homemade ginger beer. It acts as a fermenting agent and gives the drink its fizzy quality. Let's get one thing clear: There is bad yeast (not worth describing here) and then there is the beneficial kind, typically from the Saccharomyces *genus, which has anti-microbial effects in the gut. Active dried yeast is absolutely paleo-friendly and is used in this drink. This is a quick version that takes only 24 hours.*

MAKES 4 CUPS

4 cups boiling water

½ cup raw honey

Zest and juice of 1 lemon, plus lemon wedges for serving

⅔ cup peeled and sliced ginger

1 tsp active dry yeast

Ice cubes for serving

Mint leaves for serving

Let the boiled water cool slightly, so it's okay to touch. In a large bowl, combine the water, honey, lemon zest, lemon juice, ginger, and yeast. Cover loosely with muslin or plastic wrap. Set aside at room temperature for 24 hours.

With a slotted spoon, skim off any scum that has risen to the surface. Strain the liquid through a fine-mesh sieve and pour into clean glass bottles or jars (leave a little room at the top). Store, refrigerated, for up to 2 months. Serve over ice with lemon wedges and mint.

strawberry kisses

If using frozen strawberries, rinse them under hot water to thaw.

MAKES 1 TO 1½ CUPS

6 strawberries, stemmed

⅔ cup coconut milk

1 tsp almond butter

½ tsp vanilla extract

½ cup ice cubes

In a blender, combine the strawberries, coconut milk, almond butter, vanilla, and ice and blend into a smooth, thick purée. Pour into glasses and serve immediately.

raspberry gin fizz

This cocktail is inspired by a drink I used to make during my cocktail days. You could use vodka instead of gin and strawberries instead of raspberries. Chambord is a French raspberry liqueur but you could use another good-quality variety.

MAKES 1 CUP PURÉE

For the raspberry purée

½ cup raspberries

½ cup water

1 tsp raw honey or other natural sweetener

For each cocktail

2 Tbsp good-quality gin

2 Tbsp Chambord liqueur

¼ cup raspberry purée (above)

½ tsp vanilla extract

1 Tbsp lemon juice

Ice cubes

½ cup soda water

1 or 2 small mint sprigs

A few raspberries

To make the raspberry purée: In a blender, combine the raspberries, water, and honey and blend to a smooth purée. Store, refrigerated, in a squeeze bottle.

To make one cocktail: In a cocktail shaker, combine the gin, Chambord, raspberry purée, vanilla, lemon juice, and a handful of ice. Shake well and strain as you pour over fresh ice cubes in a tumbler. Top with the soda water and garnish with mint and raspberries. Serve immediately.

Thanks

This cookbook was made possible with the support of many friends, and strangers. Whether you were with me through the whole process or helped out on occasion by cleaning up my kitchen mess and testing my food, I want to thank you from the bottom of my heart.

Special mention to some of my close friends and loved ones who had to put up with me for the last few months.

Matti Puckridge, Carla Hackett, Jodie McLeod, Tim Lucas, Gloria Tong, Stephen Lead, Simon Wright, Lilli Altendorfer, Ursula Everett, Eric Auld, Melody Puckridge, Elle Patrikis, Danielle Szetho, and my family.

And a huge thank you to all my Pozible supporters.

Alison Mitchell
Andrew Wyers
Anna
Annalea Johnston
Annette Boehm
Ben Askins
Ben Webster
Bruno Mattarollo
Cameron Barrie
Caroline Strudwick-Brown
Cate Prentice
Chris Stephens
Cyrus Eftos
Danielle Szetho
Deb Davidson
Deborah Caddy
Dmitry Baranovskiy
Enrique Salceda
Evan Ford
Freya Davidson
Garmisch & Tim Riley
Gemma Starzec
Gloria Tong
Hayli Chwang
Inna Yankevych
Jacquie Collins
Jared Wyles
Jason Crane
Jennifer Manefield
Josh Ruscheinsky

Jodi Morgan
John Rimmer
Julie Keith
Justin Koke
Justin Vön Ong
Kath Hamilton
Kerensa Anderson
Kris Owen
Kristian Milos
Kristina Ljubicic
Kurumi Honda
Lauren Whitehead
Leanne Barry
Lexi Thorn
Lily Perthuis
Lisa Miller
Luisa Bolzic
Magi Hernandez
Marcus Stenbeck
Marinka Bil
Mark Cowley
Matt Willis
Maxine Sherrin
Michael Koukoullis
Mychelle Vanderburg
Nadine Richter
Narelle Hickling-
    Thompson
Nathan de Vries
Nicole Smith

Patrick Cranshaw
Pauline Allen
Petter Lundmark
Rashelle Zelaznik
Rebecca Axon
Rod Tobin
Ryan Junee
Ryan Kitching
Sanna Lundmark
Shari Henderson
Sharon Worster
Simon Ratner
Simon Wright
Sophia Molodysky
Sophie Wright
Srini Madhavan
Stephen Cox
Stephen Mason-Ellen
Steve Gilles
Sue Cotterell
Sugendran Ganess
Tim Lucas
Toby Forage
Tony Hall
Trent Brown
Ursula Everett
And Niulife for yummy
    coconut goodies

references

BOOKS

Enig, Mary and Fallon, Sally. *Eat Fat, Lose Fat: The Healthy Alternative to Trans Fats.* New York: Plume, 2006.

Fallon, Sally. *Nourishing Traditions: The Cookbook That Challenges Politically Correct Nutrition and the Diet Dictocrats.* Lanham: New Trends Publishing Inc, US, 2003.

Jaminet, P and Jaminet, S-C. *Perfect Health Diet: Four Steps To Renewed Health, Youthful Vitality, and Long Life.* YingYang Press, 2010.

Sanfilippo, Diane. *Practical Paleo: A Customised Approach to Health and a Whole-foods Lifestyle.* Las Vegas: Victory Belt Publishing, 2012.

Wolf, Robb. *The Paleo Solution: The Original Human Diet.* Las Vegas: Victory Belt Publishing, 2010.

ONLINE RESOURCES

Ballantyne, S, 2012, *The Science and Art of Paleofying—Part 1 Paleo Flours,* accessed 17 March, 2013

Ballantyne, S, 2012, *The Autoimmune Protocol,* accessed 18 March, 2013

Byrnes, S, 2002, *Myths of Vegetarianism,* accessed 20 March, 2013

Carrera-Bastos P, Fontes Villalba M, O'Keefe JH, Lindeberg S, Cordain L, 2011, *The Western Diet and Lifestyle and Diseases of Civilization,* PDF, accessed 24 March, 2013

Crawford, A, 2013, *Activating Nuts and Seeds,* accessed 19 March 2013

Eades, M.R., 2009, *Nutrition and health in agriculturalists and hunter-gatherers,* accessed 15 December, 2012

Eaton SB, Cordain L, Sparling PB, Cantwell JD., 2009, *Evolution, Body Composition and Insulin Resistance,* PDF, accessed 24 March, 2013

Johnson, K, 2013, *Health Benefits of Bone Broth,* accessed 3 March, 2013

Kresser, C, 2012, *Shaking up The Salt Myth: When Salt Reduction May Be Warranted,* accessed 15 December, 2012

Kresser, C, 2013, *Does Red Meat Cause Inflammation?,* accessed 15 April, 2013

Kresser, C, 2013, *Red Meat: It Does a Body Good,* accessed 23 March, 2012

Lindeberg, S, Jönsson, T, Granfeldt, Y, Borgstrand, E, Soffman, J, Sjöström, K, and Ahrén, B, 2007, *A Palaeolithic diet improves glucose tolerance more than a Mediterranean-like diet in individuals with ischaemic heart disease,* accessed 17 March, 2013

Taylor, J, n.d., *Paleo Diet Carbohydrate List and Carb Counter,* accessed 18 March, 2013

Satin, M, 2012, *Salt and Our Health,* accessed 16 March, 2013

Sisson, M, 2009, *The Primal Blueprint Carbohydrate Curve,* accessed 19 March, 2013

Wolf, Robb. 2013, *What is the Paleo Diet?,* accessed 20 January, 2013

Myths & Truths About Nutrition, 2000, accessed 18 March, 2013

It's the Beef, 2000, accessed 13 February, 2013

Grains & Legumes

Freed, D.L.J., 1999, *Do Dietary Lectins Cause Disease?*, accessed 15 March, 2013

Jaminet, P, 2010, *Wheat Is A Cause of Many Diseases, I: Leaky Gut*, accessed 16 March, 2013

Jaminet, P, 2011, *Why We Get Fat: Food Toxins*, accessed 16 March, 2013

Kresser, C, 2011, *9 Steps To Perfect Health - #1: Don't Eat Toxins*, accessed 19 December, 2013

Rose, A, 2013, *Phytic Acid*, accessed 17 March, 2013

Sgourakis, E, 2012, *Don't Go Nuts*, accessed 19 March, 2013

Less Bad but Not Good: Pseudograins and Non-Gluten Grains, n.d., accessed 17 March, 2013

Soy Alert, n.d., accessed 10 March, 2013

Sugar/Sweeteners

Appleton, N and Jacobs, G.N., 2010, *141 Reasons Sugar Ruins Your Health*, accessed 21 March, 2013

Cordain, L, n.d., *Sugar Content of Fruit*, accessed March 22, 2013

Fallon Morell, S and Nagel R, 2009, *Agave Nectar: Worse Than We Thought*, accessed 23 March, 2013

Kresser, C, 2012, *Ask Chris: Is Fructose Really That Bad?*, accessed 29 February, 2013

Sanfilippo, D, n.d., *Guide to Sweeteners*, PDF, accessed 22 March, 2013

Sisson, M, 2010, *The Definitive Guide to Sugar*, accessed 21 March, 2013

Sisson, M, 2011, *A Primal Primer: Stevia*, accessed 23 March, 2013

Fats & Oils

Champ, C.E., 2012, *Checking Your Oil: The Definitive Guide to Cooking with Fat*, accessed 22 March, 2013

Cordain, L, n.d., *Fats and Fatty Acids*, accessed 22 March, 2013

Masterjohn, C, 2012, *Good Fats, Bad Fats: Separating Facts from Fiction*, accessed 22 March, 2013

Rose, L, 2011, *The Complete Guide to Fats and Oils—What to Cook With (or not), What to Avoid and Why*, accessed 24 March, 2013

Sanfilippo, D, n.d., *Guide to Fats & Oils*, PDF, accessed March 24 2012

Sisson, M, 2008, *The Definitive Guide to Cholesterol*, accessed 22 March, 2013

Taylor, J, 2010, *Omega 6 and 3 in Nuts, Oils, Meat and Fish. Tools to Get It Right*, accessed 19 March, 2013

Myths and Truths About Cholesterol, 2009, accessed 23 March, 2013

Types of *Cooking Fats and Oils—Smoking Points of Fats and Oils, n.d.*, accessed 22 March, 2013

Dairy

Kresser, C, 2013, *For A Healthy Heart, Stick to Butter*, accessed 24 March, 2013

Kresser, C, 2011, *Dairy: Foods of The Gods or Neolithic Agent of Disease?*, accessed 24 March, 2013

Kubal, Amy, 2012, *Seven Shades of Paleo*, accessed 24 March, 2013

Sisson, M, 2009, *Is All Cheese Created Equal?*, accessed 24 March, 2013

Sisson, M, 2010, *The Definitive Guide to Dairy*, accessed 24 March, 2013

index